THE IT4IT™ REFER
VERS

A POCK

C000174480

The Open Group Publications available from Van Haren Publishing

The TOGAF Series:
TOGAF® Version 9.1
TOGAF® Version 9.1 – A Pocket Guide
TOGAF® 9 Foundation Study Guide, 3rd Edition
TOGAF® 9 Certified Study Guide, 3rd Edition

The Open Group Series:
The IT4IT™ Reference Architecture, Version 2.1
IT4IT™ for Managing the Business of IT – A Management Guide
IT4IT™ Foundation Study Guide
The IT4IT™ Reference Architecture, Version 2.1 – A Pocket Guide
Cloud Computing for Business – The Open Group Guide
ArchiMate® 3.0 – A Pocket Guide
ArchiMate® 2 Certification – Study Guide
ArchiMate® 3.0 Specification

The Open Group Security Series:
O-TTPS - A Management Guide
Open Information Security Management Maturity Model (O-ISM3)
Open Enterprise Security Architecture (O-ESA)
Risk Management – The Open Group Guide
The Open FAIR™ Body of Knowledge – A Pocket Guide

All titles are available to purchase from:
www.opengroup.org
www.vanharen.net
and also many international and online distributors.

The IT4IT™ Reference Architecture, Version 2.1

A POCKET GUIDE

Prepared by Andrew Josey et al.

Title:	The IT4IT™ Reference Architecture, Version 2.1 – A Pocket Guide
Series:	The Open Group Series
A Publication of:	The Open Group
Author:	Andrew Josey et al.
Publisher:	Van Haren Publishing, Zaltbommel, www.vanharen.net
ISBN Hardcopy:	978 94 018 0 169 0
ISBN eBook:	978 94 018 0 170 6
ISBN ePUB:	978 94 018 0 171 3
Edition:	First edition, first impression, October 2015 (Version 2.0)
	Second edition, first impression, April 2017 (Version 2.1)
Layout and Cover Design:	Coco Bookmedia, Amersfoort – NL
Copyright:	© 2015, 2017 The Open Group All rights reserved.

Pocket Guide

The IT4IT™ Reference Architecture, Version 2.1 - A Pocket Guide
Document Number: G171

Published by The Open Group, April 2017.

Comments relating to the material contained in this document may be submitted to:

The Open Group
Apex Plaza
Reading
Berkshire, RG1 1AX
United Kingdom

or by electronic mail to: ogspecs@opengroup.org

Contents

Preface

This Document

This document is the Pocket Guide for the IT4IT™ Reference Architecture, Version 2.1, an Open Group Standard. It is designed to provide a reference for Business Managers, IT professionals, practitioners, and IT leaders.

The IT Value Chain and IT4IT Reference Architecture represent the IT service lifecycle in a new and powerful way. They provide the missing link between industry standard best practice guides and the technology framework and tools that power the IT service management ecosystem. The IT Value Chain and IT4IT Reference Architecture are a new foundation on which to base your IT operating model. Together, they deliver a blueprint to accelerate IT's transition to becoming a service broker to the business. They also address strategic challenges brought about by mobility, cloud, big data, security, and Bring Your Own Device (BYOD).

This allows organizations to:
- Focus on the true role of IT: to deliver services that make the company more competitive
- Support the multi-sourced service economy, enabling new experiences in driving the self-sourcing of services that power innovation

The intended audiences for this Pocket Guide include:
- Individuals who require a basic understanding of the IT Value Chain and IT4IT Reference Architecture
- IT Professionals who are responsible for delivering services in a way that is flexible, traceable, and cost-effective
- IT Professionals/Practitioners who are focused on instrumenting the IT management landscape
- IT leaders who are concerned about the nature and appropriateness of their operating model

A prior knowledge of IT service management is advantageous but not required.

The Pocket Guide is structured as follows:
- Chapter 1 provides an introduction to this Pocket Guide, the IT4IT Reference Architecture, the structure of the IT4IT standard, and the positioning of the IT4IT standard in the standards landscape
- Chapter 2 describes the IT Value Chain and IT4IT Reference Architecture concepts, including Value Streams
- Chapter 3 describes the Strategy to Portfolio (S2P) Value Stream
- Chapter 4 describes the Requirement to Deploy (R2D) Value Stream
- Chapter 5 describes the Request to Fulfill (R2F) Value Stream
- Chapter 6 describes the Detect to Correct (D2C) Value Stream
- Appendix A summarizes the differences between the IT4IT Reference Architecture and ITIL
- Appendix B includes the glossary of terms
- Appendix C includes acronyms and abbreviations used in this Pocket Guide

About the IT4IT™ Reference Architecture Standard
- The evolving IT4IT standard provides a vendor-neutral, technology-agnostic, and industry-agnostic reference architecture for managing the business of IT, enabling insight for continuous improvement
- The IT4IT standard provides the capabilities for managing the business of IT that will enable IT execution across the entire Value Chain in a better, faster, cheaper way with less risk
- The IT4IT standard is industry-independent to solve the same problems for everyone
- The IT4IT standard is designed for existing landscapes and accommodates future IT paradigms

The IT4IT Reference Architecture Standard, Version 2.1 – Release Highlights
The following topics have been included/enhanced in Version 2.1 of the IT4IT Reference Architecture:

- Service Model simplification and enhancement
  The data objects which make up the Service Model Backbone have
  been simplified and better defined to lead to a stronger understanding
  of the Reference Architecture in its entirety. The Service Model is the
  backbone of the entire standard.

- Financial Management supporting function
  The Reference Architecture has been updated to highlight how
  financial management capabilities are now supported by the standard.
  Financial Management is one of the supporting functions in the
  overall IT Value Chain and has impacts on core functions and data
  objects which have been updated to more effectively support this
  capability.

- General consistency and flow of the overall standard
  The Reference Architecture 2.0 was the first version of the
  standard which was published. There were certain sections, naming
  conventions, and content which lacked some consistency throughout
  the standard which have now been resolved.

Conventions Used in this Pocket Guide
The following conventions are used throughout this Pocket Guide in
order to help identify important information and avoid confusion over
the intended meaning.

- Ellipsis (…)
  Indicates a continuation; such as an incomplete list of example items,
  or a continuation from preceding text.
- **Bold**
  Used to highlight specific terms.
- *Italics*
  Used for emphasis. May also refer to other external documents.

In addition to typographical conventions, the following conventions are used to highlight segments of text:

 A Note box is used to highlight useful or interesting information.

About The Open Group

The Open Group is a global consortium that enables the achievement of business objectives through IT standards. With more than 500 member organizations, The Open Group has a diverse membership that spans all sectors of the IT community – customers, systems and solutions suppliers, tool vendors, integrators, and consultants, as well as academics and researchers – to:

- Capture, understand, and address current and emerging requirements, and establish policies and share best practices
- Facilitate interoperability, develop consensus, and evolve and integrate specifications and open source technologies
- Offer a comprehensive set of services to enhance the operational efficiency of consortia
- Operate the industry's premier certification service

Further information on The Open Group is available at www.opengroup.org.

The Open Group publishes a wide range of technical documentation, most of which is focused on development of Open Group Standards and Guides, but which also includes white papers, technical studies, certification and testing documentation, and business titles. Full details and a catalog are available at www.opengroup.org/bookstore.

Readers should note that updates – in the form of Corrigenda – may apply to any publication. This information is published at www.opengroup.org/corrigenda.

About the Authors

The individuals in this section contributed to the development of this Pocket Guide. For contributors to the standard, please see the Acknowledgements section.

Andrew Josey, The Open Group
Andrew Josey is Vice-President, Standards and Certification, overseeing all certification and testing programs at The Open Group. He also manages the standards process for The Open Group. Since joining the company in 1996, Andrew has been closely involved with the standards development, certification, and testing activities of The Open Group.

Rob Akershoek, Logicalis SMC
Rob Akershoek is an IT management architect working for Logicalis SMC and currently the chair of the IT4IT Forum. He has been involved in the IT4IT Reference Architecture from the start in his role as IT4IT architect at Shell. He has been working on IT management for 20 years.

Charles (Charlie) Betz, Armstrong Process Group
Charlie Betz is the founder of Digital Management Academy LLC, a training, advisory, and consulting firm. He spent six years at Wells Fargo as VP and Enterprise Architect for IT Portfolio Management and Systems Management. He has held analyst, architect, and application manager positions for AT&T, Best Buy, Target, EMA, and Accenture, specializing in IT management, Cloud, and Enterprise Architecture. Currently, he is active in The Open Group IT4IT Forum representing Armstrong Process Group.

Christopher Davis, University of South Florida
Christopher Davis is Professor of Information Systems at the University of South Florida. His academic career spans 26 years, prior to which he spent 18 years in roles as an analyst and project manager in public sector

and corporate organizations in the UK and Europe. Chris is a former Chairman of The Open Group IT4IT Forum.

Sue Desiderio, PricewaterhouseCoopers LLP, USA

Sue Desiderio is an IT Director within the IT Enablement organization at PwC. She has been part of the IT4IT initiative from the beginning with a focus on the service model and the Requirement to Deploy value stream. She has worked to continuously improve the business of IT for internal IT organizations over the last 18 years.

Sylvain Marie, Arismore

Sylvain Marie is Project Director and Lead IT4IT Architect at Arismore, a consulting company involved in digital transformation. He is a member of itSMF, The Open Group IT4IT Forum, and is ITIL and TOGAF certified. Within the itSMF, he is co-author of a white paper on "Transforming IT into a Service Provider" and has recently led a work stream on "Architecting the Information System of IT".

David Morlitz, IBM

David Morlitz is an Executive Client Architect at IBM with a focus on z Systems (mainframe) technologies. He has worked with companies for over 15 years to design innovative software solutions to improve business efficiency and add new functionality to existing applications. He holds a degree in economics and an MBA, which allow him to bring strong business value to IT projects. He is certified both as a Master Certified Architect and Distinguished IT Specialist through The Open Group.

Lars Rossen, Hewlett Packard Enterprise

Lars Rossen is a Distinguished Technologist, and Chief Architect of the IT4IT initiative in Hewlett Packard Enterprise (HPE). He was part of the inception of the IT4IT initiative and constructed the first version of the IT4IT architecture. He leads the initiative that aligns and integrates all of the HPE management tools using the IT4IT standard as the reference. Lars has been working on IT and Service Provider

management systems and software for 20 years. Lars has a PhD in
Computer Science, an MSc in Engineering, and an MBA in Technology
Management. He currently lives in Denmark.

Trademarks

ArchiMate®, DirecNet®, Making Standards Work®, OpenPegasus®, The Open Group®, TOGAF®, UNIX®, UNIXWARE®, X/Open®, and the Open Brand X® logo are registered trademarks and Boundaryless Information Flow™, Build with Integrity Buy with Confidence™, Dependability Through Assuredness™, EMMM™, FACE™, the FACE™ logo, IT4IT™, the IT4IT™ logo, O-DEF™, O-PAS™, Open FAIR™, Open Platform 3.0™, Open Process Automation™, Open Trusted Technology Provider™, Platform 3.0™, SOSA™, the Open O™ logo, and The Open Group Certification logo (Open O and check™) are trademarks of The Open Group.

CMMI® is registered in the US Patent and Trademark Office by Carnegie Mellon University.

COBIT® is a registered trademark of the Information Systems Audit and Control Association (ISACA) and the IT Governance Institute.

eTOM® is a registered trademark of the TM Forum.

ITIL® is a registered trademark of AXELOS Ltd.

OASIS™ and TOSCA™ are trademarks of OASIS.

Unified Modeling Language® and UML® are registered trademarks of the Object Management Group, Inc. in the United States and/or other countries.

All other brands, company, and product names are used for identification purposes only and may be trademarks that are the sole property of their respective owners.

Acknowledgements

The Open Group gratefully acknowledges past and present members of The Open Group IT4IT™ Forum for developing the IT4IT Reference Architecture and additional associated materials, including at the time of publication:

Steering Committee
- Rob Akershoek, Logicalis SMC, Chair
- Mike Fulton, Nationwide, Vice-Chair
- Linda Kavanagh, The Open Group, Forum Director
- Andrew Josey, The Open Group, VP Standards & Certification
- Cathy Fox, The Open Group, Technical Editor

Lead Architects
- Core Group: Lars Rossen, Hewlett Packard Enterprise
- Service Model Management: Sue Desiderio, PricewaterhouseCoopers LLP, USA
- IT Financial Management: Philippe Geneste, Accenture
- IT Asset Management: Charlie Betz, Armstrong Process Group
- Service-Level Management: Ohad Goldfarb, Hewlett Packard Enterprise

Lead Value Stream Editors
- Core: Lars Rossen, Hewlett Packard Enterprise
- S2P: Jim Johnson, Hewlett Packard Enterprise
- R2D: Sue Desiderio, PricewaterhouseCoopers LLP, USA
- R2F: Dan Rosenzweig, Hewlett Packard Enterprise
- D2C: Ohad Goldfarb, Hewlett Packard Enterprise

Reviewers
The Open Group gratefully acknowledges the following reviewers of this document:
- Steve Else

- Mike Fulton
- Ohad Goldfarb
- Steve Philp
- Ryan Schmierer
- Mark Smalley
- Bart Verbrugge
- Erik Witte

References

The following documents are referenced in this Pocket Guide:

- ArchiMate® 3.0 Specification, an Open Group Standard (C162), June 2016, published by The Open Group; refer to: www.opengroup.org/bookstore/catalog/c162.htm
- M. Porter: Competitive Advantage: Creating and Sustaining Superior Performance, ISBN: 978-0684841465, Free Press; 1st Edition (June 1998)
- TOGAF® Version 9.1 (English version), an Open Group Standard, available online at www.opengroup.org/architecture/togaf9-doc/arch, and also available as TOGAF Version 9.1 "The Book" (ISBN: 978 90 8753 6794, G116) at www.opengroup.org/bookstore/catalog/g116.htm

Chapter 1
Introduction

This Pocket Guide provides a first introduction to the IT4IT Reference Architecture, Version 2.1, an Open Group Standard. It will be of interest to individuals who require a basic understanding of the IT4IT Reference Architecture, and IT professionals and IT leaders who are concerned with – or about – their operating model.

This chapter provides a brief overview of the standard.

Topics addressed in this chapter include:
- An introduction to the IT4IT Reference Architecture
- The benefits of using the IT4IT Reference Architecture
- The structure and constituent parts of the IT4IT Reference Architecture
- The relationship of the IT4IT standard to other Open Group standards and to other industry frameworks and methodologies

1.1 An Introduction to the IT4IT Reference Architecture

The Open Group IT4IT Reference Architecture standard is a standard reference architecture for managing the business of IT. It uses a value chain approach to create a model of the functions that IT performs to help organizations identify the activities that contribute to business competitiveness. The standard serves the digital enterprise with support for real-world use-cases (e.g., Cloud-sourcing, Agile, DevOps, and service brokering) as well as embracing and complementing existing process frameworks and methodologies (e.g., ITIL®, COBIT®, SAFe, and the TOGAF® standard).

It offers great value to any company that takes managing the business of IT seriously, and especially those with an interest in business and IT transitions. It allows the IT function within an organization to achieve the same level of business discipline, predictability, and efficiency as other functions in the business.

The standard is focused on defining, sourcing, consuming, and managing IT services by looking holistically at the entire IT Value Chain. While existing frameworks and standards have placed their main emphasis on process, this standard is process-agnostic, focused instead on the data needed to manage a service through its lifecycle. It then describes the functional components (software) that are required to produce and consume the data. Once integrated together, a system of record fabric for IT management is created that ensures full visibility and traceability of the service from cradle to grave.

The IT4IT standard provides an Information Model
It is important to understand that the IT4IT Reference Architecture is not a process model; it is complementary to process models. It is an information model based on the concept of an IT Value Chain that models the functions that IT performs.

The IT4IT standard is neutral with respect to development and delivery models. It is intended to support Agile as well as waterfall approaches, and Lean Kanban process approaches as well as fully elaborated IT service management process models.

1.2 Why Use the IT4IT Reference Architecture?

The following are key reasons to use IT4IT Reference Architecture standard:

- It provides a vendor-neutral, technology-agnostic, and industry-agnostic reference architecture for managing the business of IT, enabling insight for continuous improvement
- It provides the capabilities for managing the business of IT that enable IT execution across the entire Value Chain in a better, faster, cheaper way with less risk
- It is industry-independent to solve the same problems for everyone

- It is designed for existing landscapes and accommodates future IT paradigms

1.3 The Structure of the IT4IT Reference Architecture

The IT4IT Reference Architecture is built around the concept of a value chain – the IT Value Chain (see Figure 1). The IT Value Chain is a series of activities that IT performs to add value to a business service. The reference architecture (see Figure 2) encompasses the four major IT value streams from the IT Value Chain.

What is a Value Chain?
A sequence of activities required to design, produce, and provide a specific good or service, and along which information, materials, and worth flows. See also Chapter 2.

1.3.1 The IT Value Chain

The IT4IT Reference Architecture is organized around the IT Value Chain, with four value streams supported by the reference architecture.

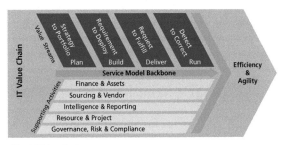

Figure 1: The IT Value Chain

The four value streams are:
- Strategy to Portfolio
- Requirement to Deploy
- Request to Fulfill
- Detect to Correct

Each IT Value Stream is centered on a key aspect of the service model, the essential data objects (information model), and functional components (functional model) that support it. Together, the four value streams play a vital role in helping IT control the service model as it advances through its lifecycle.

For more detail on the IT Value Chain see Section 2.1.

1.3.1.1 The Strategy to Portfolio (S2P) Value Stream

The **Strategy to Portfolio** (S2P) Value Stream receives strategic demands for new or improved services from the business or IT itself and develops the Conceptual Service to represent the new or enhanced service that is requested. The Conceptual Service is the bridge between business and IT in that it provides the business context for the service along with the high-level architectural attributes. For further detail see Chapter 3.

1.3.1.2 The Requirement to Deploy (R2D) Value Stream

The **Requirement to Deploy** (R2D) Value Stream receives the Conceptual Service and designs and develops the Logical Service with more detailed requirements that describe how the newly requested service and its components shall be designed. The Logical Service can be thought of as a user-friendly name for the "service system" to be created/ enhanced which delivers the value to the business. The Logical Service and designs lead to the creation of a Service Release which is further described in Service Release Blueprints which ultimately describe how the service will be instantiated when delivered. The R2D Value Stream sources (builds, buys, or rents), tests, and delivers the deployable service (Service Release Blueprint) to the R2F Value Stream. For further detail see Chapter 4.

1.3.1.3 The Request to Fulfill (R2F) Value Stream

The **Request to Fulfill** (R2F) Value Stream receives the Service Release Blueprint and creates Service Catalog Entries which represent how the service is technically delivered. Service owners build out Offers based on what technical capabilities (Service Catalog Entries) are available. The Offers are viewable to the consumer and can be ordered for a set price and service contract as detailed in the Offer. Once ordered, the R2F Value Stream is responsible for the tasks to transition the service into production where the D2C Value Stream picks up the operational activities of the service. For further details see Chapter 5.

1.3.1.4 The Detect to Correct (D2C) Value Stream

The **Detect to Correct** (D2C) Value Stream provides a framework for integrating the monitoring, management, remediation, and other operational aspects associated with realized services and/or those under construction. It also provides a comprehensive overview of the business of IT operations and the services these teams deliver. Output from the D2C Value Stream enters the lifecycle as new demands within the S2P Value Stream. For further details see Chapter 6.

1.3.2 The IT4IT Reference Architecture

The IT4IT Reference Architecture supports the IT Value Chain. It provides a prescriptive framework to support the value chain-based IT organization and service-centric IT management ecosystem. It can be considered as describing the "IT for IT" (IT4IT) architecture and relationships.

A complete, detailed IT4IT architecture would be unreadable, unmanageable, and impossible to understand. The solution is to use a layered refinement approach. Thus, the IT4IT Reference Architecture is communicated using multiple levels of abstraction. This decompositional approach is similar to that employed by other frameworks such as eTOM® from the TM Forum. Each abstraction level expands on the prior to expose more details and prescriptive guidance.

There are five levels. The upper levels (1-3) are vendor-agnostic and provide more generic views that are suitable for strategy and planning purposes as well as for creating IT management product roadmaps. The lower levels (4-5) provide more specific details, ultimately arriving at implementation level or vendor-owned/controlled information. Content at these levels is suitable for developing implementation plans and for facilitating product design. The IT4IT Reference Architecture defines five abstraction levels as depicted in Figure 2.

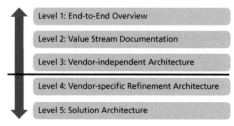

Figure 2: IT4IT Reference Architecture Levels

The standard defines Levels 1 to 3. Levels 4 and 5 are not defined by the standard, which provides example guidance only at these levels. Product and service providers implement Levels 4 and 5.

The Level 1 Architecture is shown in Figure 3, which illustrates the focus on the entire IT Value Chain; everything from help desk, data centers, end user training, and hardware infrastructure to the administrators and technicians that keep everything running as part of its Requirements to Deploy or Detect to Correct value streams. Other value streams include Strategy to Portfolio (planning) and Request to Fulfill (consumption).

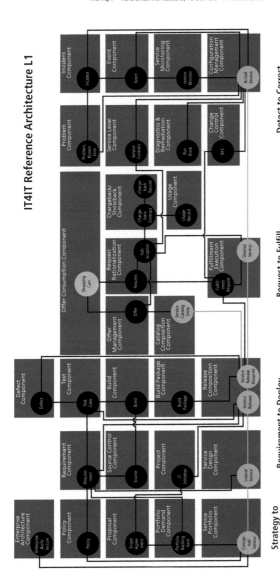

Figure 3: IT4IT Level 1 Reference Architecture Model

1.4 IT4IT Positioning

This section describes the positioning of the IT4IT Reference Architecture with respect to other Open Group standards and industry frameworks and methodologies.

1.4.1 The Need for an IT Reference Architecture

There are many standards related to IT and IT management. A careful analysis of the current landscape was carried out before the decision to develop yet another IT standard. What became apparent in the examination of the landscape was that there was indeed a gap where an IT reference architecture would fit. Mature industry verticals (e.g., retail, telecom) and professionalized management functions (e.g., finance, supply chain, HR) are evolving reference architectures, typically under some form of open consortium governance. Notable examples include:

• The work of the Association of Retail Technology Standards under the National Retail Federation (NRF/ARTS), including a comprehensive data model and process taxonomy
  This data architecture is used extensively by vendors of retail technology as a standard for product interoperability.
• Frameworx, a suite of best practices and standards from the Tele-Management Forum (TM Forum)
  Frameworx and its related standards constitute a robust, multi-view architectural representation of telecom architecture, including processes, capabilities, data, and reference systems.

1.4.2 Relationship to the TOGAF® and ArchiMate® Standards and ITIL®

Figure 4 shows the relationship of the IT4IT Reference Architecture to the TOGAF and ArchiMate standards, and also the ITIL best practice framework.

1.4.2.1 The ArchiMate® Modeling Language

The IT4IT standard uses the ArchiMate notation to specify and publish the Reference Architecture and, hence, play back the use-cases for further

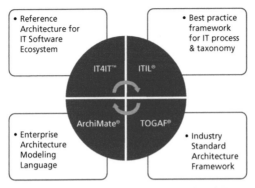

Figure 4: Relationship to the TOGAF and ArchiMate Standards and ITIL

improvement. The ArchiMate language (together with UML®) is used at abstraction Level 3 as the primary method for communicating the IT4IT Reference Architecture specification.

1.4.2.2 ITIL®

ITIL is a best practice framework focused around processes, capabilities, and disciplines. The IT4IT standard embraces ITIL as guidance in the definition of the IT Value Chain-related capabilities and process-driven dependencies. The differences between the IT4IT standard and ITIL are summarized in Appendix A.

1.4.2.3 The TOGAF® Framework

The TOGAF framework has been used to develop the IT4IT Reference Architecture: the IT4IT Value Streams and Reference Architecture thus include the Enterprise Architecture capability. The benefit here is mutual: the evolution and use of the IT4IT standard – particularly around manageability and integration – will contribute to the extension and refinement of the TOGAF framework. The TOGAF methodology fits well with the "front end" or planning side of the IT Value Chain (S2P).

1.4.3 Relationship to Other Industry Frameworks and Methods

TOSCA™, an OASIS standard, is an important emerging standard that plugs in at Level 3 (and lower) enabling specification and mapping of deployment structures from various sources.

COBIT® – provides IT capability-related KPIs as guidance for the IT4IT standard in the specification of key data artifacts.

SAFe – in general the IT4IT standard is agnostic of the development methodology chosen, agile or waterfall; the reality is almost always a mix. More importantly, the IT4IT standard is reflective and compliant with the enterprise planning levels and in-time planning methods based on queuing theory.

CMMI® – applying IT4IT guidance and definition catalyzes organizational maturity, which can be expressed using the Capability Maturity Model Integration framework from Carnegie Mellon University. There is opportunity to leverage the CMMI process to define a specific IT4IT maturity level, and *vice versa*: to articulate IT4IT value stream achievements as measurable criteria associated with specific maturity levels.

Chapter 2
Basic IT4IT Concepts

This chapter describes the basic concepts of the IT4IT Reference Architecture.

This chapter includes:
- The IT Value Chain and IT Value Streams
- The IT4IT Reference Architecture
- IT Service

2.1 The IT Value Chain and IT Value Streams

A value chain is a series of activities that an organization performs in order to deliver something valuable, such as a product or service. Products pass through activities of a chain in order, and at each activity the product gains some value. A value chain framework helps organizations to identify the activities that are especially important for competitiveness – for the advancement of strategy and attainment of goals.

The IT Value Chain is grouped into two main categories of activities:
- Primary activities, which are concerned with the production or delivery of goods or services for which a business function, like IT, is directly accountable
- Supporting activities, which facilitate the efficiency and effectiveness of the primary activities

Value accrues through improvements in process efficiency and agility (as shown in Figure 1).[1]

---

[1] For more on the value chain concept, see the referenced M. Porter: Competitive Advantage: Creating and Sustaining Superior Performance.

With services as the center of gravity, a value chain-based model for IT has been constructed by identifying the critical activities associated with the planning, sourcing, delivery, and management of services. The IT Value Chain content details the series of activities that every IT organization performs that add value to a business service or IT service. The IT4IT Reference Architecture breaks these activities down further to a Service Model and the essential functional components and data objects that IT produces or consumes in the IT Value Chain in order to advance the service lifecycle.

The IT4IT standard breaks down the IT Value Chain into four (4) value streams to help consumability and adoptability of the IT4IT Reference Architecture by IT organizations. Each value stream represents a key area of value that IT provides across the full service lifecycle.

The functional components in the IT Value Chain are grouped into four primary IT value streams and five supporting activities.

The four primary value streams are shown in Figure 5 and are as follows:
• Strategy to Portfolio
• Requirement to Deploy
• Request to Fulfill
• Detect to Correct

Figure 5: Value Stream Overview

The primary value streams for the IT Value Chain generally align to what IT traditionally calls "Plan, Build, Deliver, Run". When used with an IT Value Chain-based model this is transformed into "Plan, Source, Offer, and Manage". These value streams are core to the IT function and have a vital role in helping to holistically run the full service lifecycle. These are usually hosted within IT.

The five supporting activities (as shown in Figure 1) for the IT Value Chain are:
- Governance Risk & Compliance
- Sourcing & Vendor
- Intelligence & Reporting
- Finance & Assets
- Resource & Project

The supporting activities help ensure the efficiency and effectiveness of the IT Value Chain and primary value streams. These can be corporate or administrative functions that are hosted in the lines of business and/or IT.

2.2 The IT4IT Reference Architecture

The IT Value Chain is the series of activities that IT performs to add value to a business service or IT service. These activities are embodied in four value streams that provide a whole-of-life mapping for the business of IT, allowing executive managers to quickly engage in strategic and operational decision-making. The value streams, like the reference architecture, are process-agnostic, accommodating the full range of process models while maintaining overall cohesion and integrity.

The IT4IT Reference Architecture breaks down the activities in the IT Value Chain into four key pillars for IT:
1. The Service Model
2. The Information Model

3. The Functional Model
4. The Integration Model

Together these provide the prescription for the essential elements that IT must control to manage a service through its lifecycle.

Each IT Value Stream is centered on an essential element of the Service Model (see Section 2.2.1) and the configuration of key data objects (see Section 2.2.2, the Information Model), and functional components (see Section 2.2.3, the Functional Model) that support it.

2.2.1 The Service Model

Without a clear understanding of both the business and technology attributes of a service, there is no way to be certain that the desired outcome can be consistently attained and that the most optimal sourcing strategy will be applied. The Service Model construct in the architecture captures, connects, and maintains these service lifecycle attributes as the service progresses through its lifecycle.

Traditional IT lifecycles are oriented around projects, used to govern technology deployments. Therefore, the plan, build, run lifecycle is the stalwart for most IT organizations and very little data is captured and maintained for a service. The provider/broker model for the new style of IT places its focus on services as the primary IT deliverable and requires a higher degree of flexibility, velocity, and adaptability. A service-centric lifecycle framework is one that supports a continuous cycle of assessing the portfolio, sourcing and integrating components, and offering services to consumers. This requires greater degrees of control over the data associated with a service in its various stages.

The structure that binds the different abstraction levels of the Service Model together is called the "Service Model Backbone" (shown in Figure 6). The Service Model Backbone provides the data entities, attributes, and necessary relationships between them to ensure end-to-end

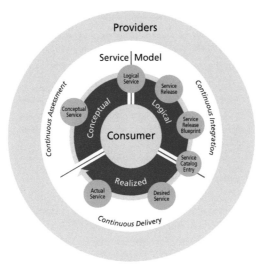

Figure 6: IT4IT Service Model

traceability of a service from concept to instantiation and consumption. This means that using this data-driven, model-based approach will ensure that what is required is actually what gets delivered or, in other words, what is offered will produce the outcome that the consumer desires. Further, it allows the IT organization to effectively utilize a service-centric approach in creating and packaging its deliverables. This requires the creation of services from across resource and capability domains such as infrastructure, application components, database, middleware, monitoring, support, and so on. This enables the organization to improve their speed and consistency through higher re-use of pre-existing services and to embrace new technologies such as containers and micro-services in a more effective manner.

2.2.2 The Information Model
The Information Model comprises the set of service lifecycle data objects and their relationships.

It is important to understand the interactions between the processes that are executed to support IT and the underpinning systems that enable these processes, as well as the information that is exchanged between these systems as the process is run. The IT4IT standard adopts a novel perspective – that the Information Model and the systems (in terms of essential services that the components deliver) should be the basis for managing IT. This provides cohesion but without dictating process methods. Processes can evolve and be optimized and, depending on the situation, different processes or process models may be chosen and used.

The components and the data artifacts that they control and exchange must be highly dependable for effective IT management: the IT4IT Reference Architecture provides that foundation. Abstraction of the IT4IT Reference Architecture into process levels maintains conceptual cohesion and integrity but allows processes to be replaced, enabling IT organizations to make consistent long-term investment in IT management solutions. This also enables the IT organization to interact consistently with its suppliers and – even more importantly – enables the IT organization to gain deep and detailed insight into how well IT is performing and contributing to the business of which it is a part.

A similar "upwards" cohesion is enabled by the IT4IT standard. The four value streams provide a whole-of-life mapping for the business of IT. This perspective is similarly process-agnostic. Its derivation from the ubiquitous value chain makes it immediately familiar to executives and provides a similarly coherent basis for strategic and operational decision-making.

The IT4IT standard fills the persistent "vacuum" between strategy and governance frameworks and tools at the highest level and tool-specific architectural components at the operational level.

Each value stream produces and/or consumes data that together represents all of the information required to control the activities that

advance a service through its lifecycle. This data has been referred to as
"service lifecycle *data objects*" (data objects in short form). Some data
objects contribute directly to creating and/or advancing the Service
Model while others serve as connectors, providing the linkage between
functional components and across value streams.

Data objects have the following characteristics:
- They describe an aspect of a service
- They are inputs or outputs associated with an IT4IT functional
  component or a service lifecycle phase
- They are uniquely identified, and have a lifecycle of their own
- They maintain structured information that allows for relationship
  tracking and automation

Service lifecycle data objects in the IT4IT Reference Architecture are
grouped into two categories: *key* and *auxiliary*.

Data Object Type	Description	Symbol
Key Data Objects	Key data objects describe aspects of "how" services are created, delivered, and consumed; they are essential to managing the service lifecycle. Managing the end-to-end service lifecycle and associated measurement, reporting, and traceability would be virtually impossible without them. The IT4IT Reference Architecture defines 32 key data objects and most are depicted as black circles.	●

Data Object Type	Description	Symbol
	Service models are a stand-alone subclass of key data objects that describe "what" IT delivers to its consumers. They represent the attributes of a service at three levels of abstraction: Conceptual, Logical, and Realized. These data objects are referred to as Service Model Backbone data objects (or service backbone data objects in short form) and depicted in this Pocket Guide using a light blue circle in the IT4IT Reference Architecture diagrams. Note that the Logical Service Model is subdivided into a Design part, a Release part, and a Consumable part. Similarly, the Realized data object is represented with both a Desired and an Actual model part.	●
Auxiliary Data Objects	Auxiliary data objects provide context for the "why, when, where, etc." attributes and, while they are important to the IT function, they *do not play a vital role in managing the service lifecycle*. The IT4IT Reference Architecture currently describes eight (8) auxiliary data objects and they are depicted using a gray colored circle.	●

The essential relationships between data objects within and across value streams are defined in the IT4IT Reference Architecture and summarized in Chapter 3 through Chapter 6 of this Pocket Guide. These relationships function as a prescriptive guide for ensuring the integrity of the Service Model as it progresses through its lifecycle and facilitate traceability across value streams.

Relationships
The IT4IT Reference Architecture provides only the essential relationships and recognizes that there are other relationships that can exist but those are not part of the prescriptive guide.

Within the IT4IT Reference Architecture, the relationship between data objects is annotated as follows:

- 1 to 1 (1:1)
  Implies that if there is a relationship, it is between two data objects. It does not imply that there will always be a relationship. For example, Events without Incidents or Incidents without Events are legitimate scenarios.
- 1 to many (1:n)
  Implies that one data object relates (A) to one or more other data objects (B...) in scenarios where there is a relationship.
- Many to many (n:m)
  Implies that both A and B above can relate to zero, one, or many of the connected data objects.

Figure 7 provides an example of the relationship notation. The relationships and notation used here are for illustration purposes only and do not reflect the actual notation used or the relationship between the specific data objects shown.

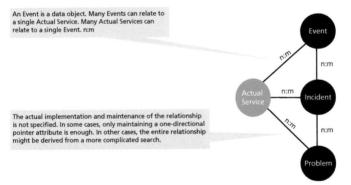

Figure 7: Data Objects and Relationships

Multiplicity Notation
In the IT4IT Reference Architecture notation, the multiplicity is always written horizontally (e.g., 1:1 in Figure 7). In some cases, the related entities are depicted vertically. When this occurs the general rules of mathematics should be applied to determine the relationship. This means the left position number/letter relates to the entity that is left or upward and the right position number/letter relates to the entity right or downward.

2.2.3 The Functional Model

The IT4IT Reference Architecture identifies and defines one of the essential building blocks – functional components – that create or consume data objects and can be aligned with the appropriate value streams. These functional components are based on real IT scenarios and use-cases.

The context for functional components starts with an IT "capability". A capability is the ability that an organization, person, or system possesses (function or activity it can perform) which produces an outcome of value through the utilization of a combination of people, process, methods, technology resources, and/or tools.

Functional components can be logically associated to IT capabilities for organizational clarity and underpinned with processes to drive uniformity and consistency.

A functional component is the smallest technology unit that can stand on its own and be useful as a whole to a customer. Functional components have defined input(s) and output(s) that are data objects and impact on a key data object (for example, a state change). Functional components typically control a single data object. A grouping of one or more functional components represents the technology elements of an IT capability.

Capturing the architecture in this manner and constructing the eco-system using this approach delivers on the agility promise and ensures end-to-end traceability by focusing on data rather than process as the design guide. Processes can change, organizational structures can shift (such as centralized/decentralized), and yet the Information Model remains constant and the architectural integrity of the IT management ecosystem is not compromised.

2.2.3.1 Functional Component Overview

Functional components are grouped into two categories: *primary* and *secondary*. These are also referred to as "key" and "auxiliary", respectively.

Functional Component Type	Description	Symbol
Primary Functional Component	A primary (key) functional component is depicted using a blue colored rectangle and is core to a specific value stream. This means that the functional component plays a key role in the activities of a particular value stream. Without this functional component, the integrity of the data objects and thus the Service Model could not be maintained consistently and efficiently.	
Secondary Functional Component	Secondary (auxiliary) functional components are depicted in this Pocket Guide using a pale blue colored rectangle and represent some level of dependency or interaction with a value stream and its data objects. While they interact with a value stream, they are not core to it and are either primary to another value stream or supporting function or represent a capability.	

Notes
1. There a few conditions when a functional component is core to or co-owned by more than one value stream (e.g., the Change Control functional component). When this occurs, the functional component is depicted using the blue colored rectangle in each value stream.

2. There is a unique condition in the R2F Value Stream where a
   relationship exists between functional components that is user
   experience-driven rather than data-driven. This condition is shown
   using an informal notation using a gray box with a black outline, as
   depicted in Figure 8.

Figure 8: Engagement Experience Portal Functional Component

The relationships and dependencies between data objects controlled
by functional components are depicted using a solid line along with
cardinality mapping. In addition to the entity relationships, functional
components interact and exchange data to form the relationship. The
data exchange between functional components is depicted using a
dotted-line arrow to represent the direction of the flow.

Figure 9: Data Flows in the IT4IT Reference Architecture

2.2.4 The Integration Model

Integration between components in the traditional IT management
ecosystem is based on capability and processes. The interfaces needed
to accommodate the requirements associated with this approach are
largely point-to-point between products to enable automation of
inter-dependent workflows. Over time, this results in a complex web of
connections that is virtually impossible to manage, making changes to
any of the components a daunting task.

The IT4IT Reference Architecture defines an integration model with
three types of integrations. These are used for simplifying the creation of
an end-to-end IT management ecosystem using functional components.
The three types are as follows:

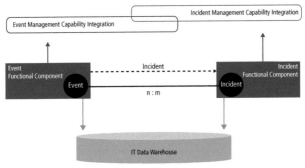

Figure 10: Engagement and Insight Information Flow

- **System of record** integrations (data-centric integration, SoR in short form)

  These entity relationship definitions ensure the consistent management of the lifecycle for individual data objects, as well as ensuring that the data objects are consistently named and cross-linked through prescriptive data flows between functional components to maintain the integrity of the Service Model. They are represented by a dotted black line like the one in Figure 10.

- **System of engagement** integrations (experience-centric integration, SoE in short form)

  These are user interface integrations derived from value stream use-cases and user stories. These integrations deliver the technology underpinning for a capability by combining several functional components into a single user experience to facilitate human interaction with data objects. In the IT4IT Reference Architecture system of engagement integrations are represented by the blue arrow in Figure 10. In the actual notation, system of engagement integrations are depicted using a dotted blue line.

- **System of insight** integrations (intelligence, analytics, and KPI-centric integrations, SoI in short form)

  These are data-centric integrations driven by the need to provide traceability, end-to-end visibility, transparency, and to capture

measurements related to services (for example, performance) or
the service lifecycle (for example, fulfillment time). Further, these
integrations can accommodate the exchange of both structured and
unstructured data that is created across the value chain. System of
insight integrations are represented by the gray arrow in Figure 10.
The actual notation for system of insight integrations has not yet been
defined as the architecture to support them will be developed in future
releases. Therefore, while this integration is mentioned here, they do
not appear in the current version documentation.

2.3 IT Service
An IT service is a performance of an act that applies computing and
information management competencies or resources for the benefit of
another party. Every IT service has three aspects: the interaction between
provider and consumer, the offer that exposes the value proposition
to consumers, and the service system which is the people, process, and
technology that facilitate the outcome.

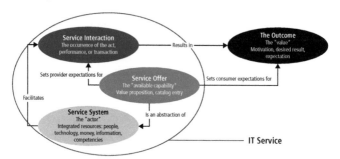

Figure 11: IT Service

These are described as follows:
• Service Interaction – an occurrence of the performance or acts where
  the computing and information competencies are applied
• Service Offer – a consumable form of an available capability that
  advertises the ability to produce or experience an outcome

It is marketed to potential consumers, defined by a contract, and (most importantly) presented in consumer-oriented terms.

- Service System – the set of integrated resources across multiple resource domains including human, financial, information, and technology that are needed to successfully implement the Service Offer and carry out the Service Interaction

Modeling and managing in this manner ensures that the appropriate people with skills/competencies, funding, information, technology components as well as other service systems remain attached to the IT service throughout its lifecycle.

Chapter 3
The S2P Value Stream

This chapter describes the Strategy to Portfolio (S2P) Value Stream.

3.1 Overview
The Strategy to Portfolio (S2P) Value Stream:
- Provides the strategy to use to balance and broker your portfolio
- Provides a unified viewpoint across PMO, Enterprise Architecture, and service portfolio
- Improves data quality for decision-making
- Provides KPIs and roadmaps to improve business communication
- Describes a lifecycle management model focused on services

The Strategy to Portfolio (S2P) Value Stream provides IT organizations with the optimal framework for interconnecting the different functions involved in managing the portfolio of services delivered to the enterprise using well-defined and consistent terminology. S2P includes activities such as capturing demand for IT services, prioritizing and forecasting investments, Service Portfolio Management, and Project Management. Using consistent terminology helps provide the necessary data consistency and transparency in order to maintain alignment between the business strategy and the IT portfolio.

Traditional IT planning and Portfolio Management activities put emphasis on capturing and tracking a collection of *projects* that represent the "orders" from the business for technology enablement. The S2P Value Stream places emphasis on the *service* and aims to provide a more holistic view of the IT portfolio to shape business investment decisions and connect IT costs with business value.

3.2 Key Value Propositions

The key value propositions for adopting the S2P Value Stream are as follows:

- Establish a holistic IT portfolio view across the IT PMO, and the Enterprise Architecture and Service Portfolio functional components so IT portfolio decisions are based on business priorities
- Use well-defined system of records between the key areas that contribute to the IT Portfolio Management function to support consistent data for accurate visibility into business and IT demand
- Endorse a Service Model that provides full service lifecycle tracking through conceptual, logical, and physical domains so it is possible to trace whether what was requested actually got delivered

3.3 Activities

Typical activities include:

Strategy	Service Portfolio	Demand	Selection
• Define objectives • Align business and IT roadmaps • Set up standards and policies	• Enterprise Architecture • Service portfolio rationalization • Create service blueprint and roadmap	• Consolidate demand • Analyze priority, urgency, and impact • Create new or tag existing demand	• Business value, risk, costs, benefits, & resources • What-if analysis • Ensure governance

Figure 12: Strategy to Portfolio Activities

The end-to-end IT portfolio view provided by the S2P Value Stream is accomplished by focusing on the service as the desired business outcome and exposing key data objects often unavailable using traditional planning methods. Defining the key data objects, the relationships between them, and their effect on the Service Models is core to the value stream approach. In addition, it provides inter-dependent functions such as Portfolio Demand, Enterprise Architecture, Service Portfolio, and Proposal functional components with data consistency and predefined data object exchanges in order to optimize the organization's IT Portfolio Management and service lifecycle management capability.

3.4 Value Stream Diagram

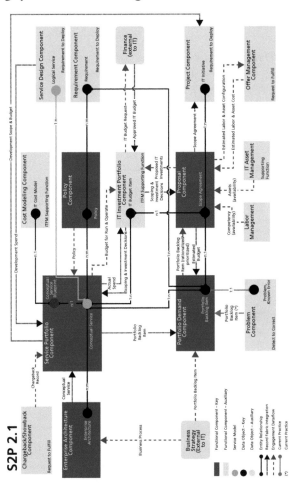

Figure 13: Strategy to Portfolio Level 2 Value Stream Diagram

3.5 Enterprise Architecture Functional Component

3.5.1 Purpose
The Enterprise Architecture functional component creates and manages long-term IT investment and execution plan-of-action that are critical to business strategic objectives.

3.5.2 Key Data Objects
The **Enterprise Architecture** data object includes references to collateral in the target state architecture landscape representing planned and deployed IT services.

The key data attributes are Id, Component, Diagram.

3.5.3 Key Data Object Relationships
Enterprise Architecture to Conceptual Service (n:m): Helps track which service components and service diagrams are allocated to which service(s).

3.5.4 Functional Criteria
The Enterprise Architecture functional component creates and manages long-term IT investment and execution plan-of-action. It identifies strategic IT architectural components based on current business vision, strategy, goals, and requirements. It develops target state business, information, application, technology, and security blueprints based on strategies, principles, and policies.

Model

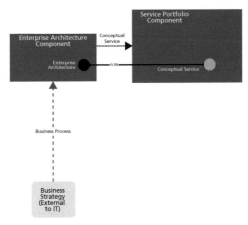

Figure 14: Enterprise Architecture Functional Component Level 2 Model

3.6 Policy Functional Component

3.6.1 Purpose
The Policy functional component manages creation, review, approval, and audit of all IT policies.

3.6.2 Key Data Objects
The **Policy** data object is a central repository for storing and organizing all types of IT policies based on various templates and classification criteria.

The key attributes are: Id, Description, ApplicableGeography.

3.6.3 Key Data Object Relationships
Policy to Conceptual Service (n:m): Multiple policies might be applicable for a single service or a single policy may be applicable for multiple services.

Policy to Requirement (n:m): Requirements may be sourced from policies or may reference policies in order to remain in compliance with previously agreed policies for an organization.

3.6.4 Functional Criteria

The Policy functional component aligns and maps IT Policies to Enterprise Architectures.

It enables review and approval of IT policies based on roles and responsibilities. It manages Policy distribution and acceptance based on predefined templates and schedules for designated IT stakeholders. It provides visibility into IT Policy attributes such as types, status, non-compliance, audit history, and issues.

It manages overall IT governance Policies, and Policies applied to or associated with the particular services that may be managed downstream during service design.

It manages IT security and regulatory Policies by incorporating external and internal security and regulatory compliances.

It defines pricing/costing Policies and captures information related to Service Contracts.

It maintains complete Policy revision history, and review period or obsolescence rules set for all Policies.

It may log and track IT Policy exceptions through an issue management mechanism. It may provide a consistent tracking feature for exception identification, evaluation, and status report leading to corrective action.

3.6.5 Data Architecture Criteria

If a Service Portfolio functional component exists, the Policy functional component associates one or more policies to one or more Conceptual Services.

Model

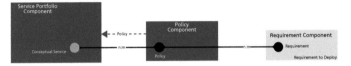

Figure 15: Policy Functional Component Level 2 Model

3.7 Proposal Functional Component

3.7.1 Purpose

The Proposal functional component manages the portfolio of IT proposals that are proposed, approved, active, deferred, or rejected.

3.7.2 Key Data Objects

The **Scope Agreement** data object reflects budget, cost/benefit projections, scope, status, and other key attributes of proposed work. The Scope Agreement is the authoritative source for the list of all IT proposals requested over a given time. It can be used for building the IT investment plan of record for the company or a specific line of business or function.

The key attributes are: Id, Description, BusinessEntity, ProposedBudget, ApprovedBudget, Status.

3.7.3 Key Data Object Relationships

Scope Agreement to Portfolio Backlog Item (n:m): One Scope Agreement can be associated to one or more demand data objects.

Scope Agreement to IT Budget Item (n:1): This relationship helps track budget allocated to which Scope Agreement.

Scope Agreement to IT Initiative (1:n): This relationship helps track IT Initiative(s) to which Scope Agreement.

3.7.4 Functional Criteria

The Proposal functional component creates a Scope Agreement from rationalized Portfolio Backlog Items in the data object repository. A Scope Agreement may follow an expedited analysis and approval for high priority urgent items or agile development proposals. A Scope Agreement may follow a structured analysis and approval via IT annual planning activities.

A Scope Agreement following an expedited analysis and approval:
- Creates a proposal from a rationalized backlog item where the item requires high urgency due to business impact on an existing service
- Allows quick evaluation of the proposal and a decision on its approval; if rejected, then it notifies the Portfolio Demand functional component
- Creates an updated Scope Agreement and updates the corresponding in-flight IT Initiative data object in the R2D Value Stream for all activities associated with a newly approved proposal
- Creates a new IT Initiative data object

Scope Agreements following a structured analysis and approval:
- Create proposals from rationalized Portfolio Backlog Items in the Portfolio Backlog Item data object repository
  Rationalized items are grouped based on priority and themes for a proposal creation purpose. Not all rationalized items will be grouped within proposals, as priority and cut-off must be decided.
- May periodically produce proposals throughout the year or once per planning period

- Create a high-level labor consumption model for a proposal (for example, one project manager, five developers, and two QAs for the proposal)
  If a Resource Management offer exists, then the Proposal functional component received the resource price from the mentioned offer. Validate labor consumption model against available internal and external labor pools.
- Create a high-level asset (non-labor) consumption model for a proposal
  If an Asset Management offer exists, then the Proposal functional component receives the asset price from the mentioned offer.
- Validate asset consumption model against available internal and external assets (for example, traditional/private cloud/managed cloud/public cloud)
- Model the ongoing labor and non-labor budget for annual and future operations
- Define tangible and intangible benefits for each proposal
  Tangible benefit may be cost savings or revenue growth, whereas intangible benefit may be strategic initiative support, competitive advantage, or compliance achieved. Work with a finance organization to validate tangible benefits. This can involve utilizing industry-specific methods of measuring the value of business processes and estimating the impact of the proposal on performance metrics.
- Ensure the proposal meets the technology policies
- Rank proposals based on benefits and risks, labor and non-labor consumption models, and ROI or other defined evaluation criteria
- May build proposal portfolio scenarios using proposals, conduct "what if" analysis on the proposal scenarios, and approve the optimal proposal scenario and its proposals
- Send proposed IT investments to the IT Investment Portfolio functional component for scoping and investment decisions
- Update Scope Agreement(s) to compare approved baseline and actual resulting benefits derived from completing the IT Initiatives

Reviews the Scope Agreement change request from the R2D Value Stream. The IT Initiative team working to deliver on the approved Scope Agreement may ask for change requests related to budget, resource, or timeline. Evaluate the change request and take action to update the existing Scope Agreement.

Considers the R2D Value Stream project portfolio as the authoritative source for the list of IT deliverables or services that will be rendered during a project lifecycle.

Creates project portfolio views for specific organizations like line of business portfolio or functions like financial views. The project portfolio is used for rationalizing and tracking resources across projects to best deliver on all projects.

Actuates the project portfolio entries through a Project Management system.

Model

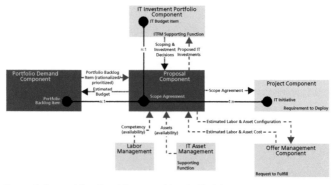

Figure 16: Proposal Functional Component Level 2 Model

The project portfolio reports back to the investment portfolio in order to accurately track progress and outcomes for a given Scope Agreement.

Identifies security controls necessary for protecting the various classifications of data.

3.8 Portfolio Demand Functional Component

3.8.1 Purpose
The Portfolio Demand functional component logs, maintains, and evaluates all demands (new service, enhancements, defects) coming into IT through a single funnel. Incoming demand received through any channel can then be categorized as correlating to similar existing demand or creating new demand.

3.8.2 Key Data Objects
The **Portfolio Backlog Item** data object represents the repository of all incoming demands including but not limited to new requests, enhancement requests, and defect fix requests.

The key attributes are: Id, Description, Source, ScopeAgreementId, EstimatedBudget, ExpectedCompletionDate, ITServiceId, FulfillmentStatus, DecisionMaker.

3.8.3 Key Data Object Relationships
Portfolio Backlog Item to Conceptual Service (n:1): One Conceptual Service may be related to one or more Portfolio Backlog Items.

Portfolio Backlog Item to Requirement (1:n): A Portfolio Backlog Item is mapped to one or more Requirements that will need to be delivered to successfully fulfill the demand.

Portfolio Backlog Item to Scope Agreement (n:1): One or more Portfolio Backlog Items may be included in a Scope Agreement.

Model

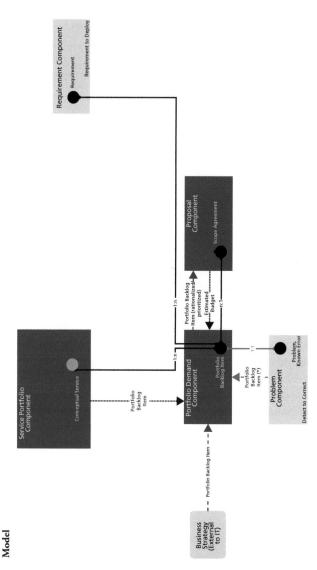

Figure 17: Portfolio Demand Functional Component Level 2 Model

3.8.4 Functional Criteria

The Portfolio Demand functional component captures Portfolio Backlog Items from business, Problem Management activities, and from the Service Portfolio functional component activities.

The Portfolio Demand functional component may capture Portfolio Backlog Items for defect fix requests, which exceed the operations budget, or require high urgency due to business impact on existing services.

The Portfolio Demand functional component may support backlog item data object backlog ranking, trending, and analysis based on requested services, timeline, business unit origination, etc.

3.9 Service Portfolio Functional Component

3.9.1 Purpose

The purpose of the Service Portfolio functional component is to manage the portfolio of services in plan, transition, production, and retirement. It is the authoritative source for the list of services that IT delivers, has delivered in the past, or brokers to itself and business. Any IT service within the Service Portfolio functional component often corresponds to one or more entries in the Offer Catalog.

3.9.2 Key Data Objects

The **Conceptual Service** (data object): Conceptual Service represents the business perspective of the service and is the service interaction or the business capability of the service. It is the level suitable for discussing aspects that characterize the service as the product of IT activity including business value, investment history and outlook, value earned, and return on investment. It is abstracted from any technical detail and described in terms that are understood by CxO-level persons who decide on the assignment of budget and resources in order to build and maintain the service.

The key attributes are: Id, Details, Owner, Status, Business Unit/Portfolio, BudgetSpend, TCO, Recovery.

The **Conceptual Service Blueprint** (auxiliary data object): The conceptual service model contains the various delivery options for a given Conceptual Service. (Each conceptual service model has a comprehensive view of the touchpoint of the multiple systems.) A service blueprint is a set of service endpoints that support business processes. A service blueprint provides service process and delivery visualization from the customer's point of view. A service blueprint also maintains traceability of Logical and Physical (realized) Service Models.

The key attributes are: Id, Details, ConceptualServiceId.

3.9.3 Key Data Object Relationships
The Conceptual Service data object:

Conceptual Service to Logical Service (1:n): Traceability is maintained between one Conceptual Service and one or more Logical Services.

Enterprise Architecture to Conceptual Service (n:m): Traceability is maintained between one or more Conceptual Services and the Enterprise Architecture drawings, diagrams, and other documents that describe those services.

Conceptual Service to Portfolio Backlog Item (1:n): One Conceptual Service may be related to one or more Portfolio Backlog Items.

Conceptual Service to IT Budget Item (1:n): Budget for one Conceptual Service may be spread across multiple budget items and one budget item should hold budget for a single Conceptual Service.

Conceptual Service to Policy (n:m): Multiple Policies might be applicable for a single service or a single Policy may be applicable for multiple services.

The Conceptual Service Blueprint data object:

Conceptual Service to Conceptual Service Blueprint (1:n): One Conceptual Service may have multiple Conceptual Service Blueprints.

IT Cost Model to Conceptual Service Blueprint (1:n): One IT cost model (rule engine) can be applicable for multiple Conceptual Service Blueprints.

Conceptual Service Blueprint to Logical Service Blueprint (1:n): One Conceptual Service Blueprint could have one or more Logical Service Blueprints.

3.9.4 Functional Criteria

The Service Portfolio functional component assesses the effectiveness and efficiency of current services delivered to business. It manages all inventory information about services or applications; including business benefits, risk, quality, fitness-for-purpose, etc. It compares similar services or applications to identify rationalization opportunities.

It evaluates the portfolio with regard to value/cost performance and risk/criticality. These methods are used to maximize portfolio value, align and prioritize resource allocations, and balance supply and demand. It reviews proposed portfolio changes; decides whether to keep, retire, or modernize services or applications.

It creates, reviews, and updates service roadmaps. It determines and tracks the TCO of a service and associated return on investment. It determines and tracks operations spend. It creates and maintains service blueprints and endpoints.

Model

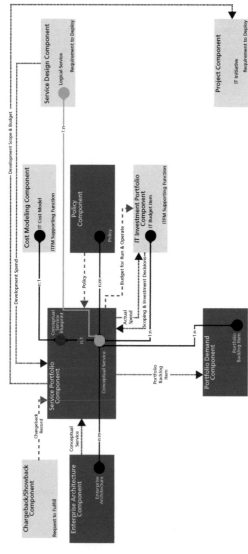

Figure 18: Service Portfolio Functional Component Level 2 Model

If a Policy exists, the Service Portfolio functional component should comply with one or more applicable Policies.

If a Chargeback/Showback functional component exists, the Service Portfolio will receive the subscribed service charge.

3.9.5 Data Architecture Criteria
The Service Portfolio functional component associates a Conceptual Service to one or more Portfolio Backlog items.

3.10 IT Investment Portfolio – Auxiliary Functional Component

3.10.1 Purpose
The IT Investment Portfolio functional component is auxiliary to the S2P Value Stream and is primary in the IT Financial Management guidance document. Its main purpose is to manage the portfolio of all IT investments.

3.10.2 Key Data Objects
The **IT Budget Item** data object is an authoritative list of approved IT investment pertaining to a service. This set of records will help to identify approved budget over different time periods; e.g., by financial year, by Conceptual Service.

The key attributes are: FinancialPeriod, InvestmentId, InvestmentType, ApprovedBudget, Spend.

3.10.3 Key Data Object Relationships
IT Budget Item to Conceptual Service (n:1): One IT Budget Item shall hold budget for a single Conceptual Service and budget for one Conceptual Service may be spread across multiple IT Budget Items.

Model

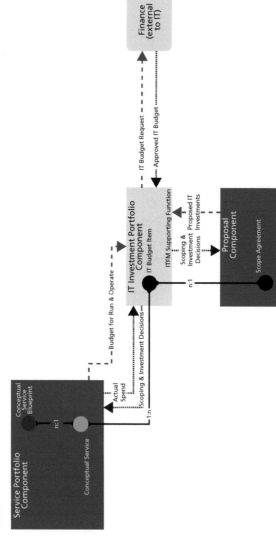

Figure 19: IT Investment Portfolio Auxiliary Functional Component Level 2 Model

IT Budget Item to Scope Agreement (1:n): This relationship helps track how much IT budget is allocated to which Scope Agreement(s).

3.10.4 Functional Criteria

The IT Investment Portfolio functional component is the authoritative system of records for all IT investments over time. It manages the entire IT investment lifecycle. It receives proposed IT investments for development from the Proposal functional component. It receives proposed IT investments for running, maintaining, and non-service investments from investment owners. It communicates the status of the final scoping and investment decisions back to the respective stakeholders.

Chapter 4
The R2D Value Stream

This chapter describes the Requirement to Deploy (R2D) Value Stream.

4.1 Overview
The Requirement to Deploy (R2D) Value Stream:
- Provides a framework for creating, modifying, or sourcing a service
- Supports agile and traditional development methodologies
- Enables visibility of the quality, utility, schedule, and cost of the services you deliver
- Defines continuous integration and deployment control points

The Requirement to Deploy (R2D) Value Stream provides the framework for creating/sourcing new services or modifying those that already exist. The goal of the R2D Value Stream is to ensure predictable, cost-effective, high quality results. It promotes high levels of re-use and the flexibility to support multi-sourcing. The R2D Value Stream is process-agnostic in that, while methods and processes may change, the functional components and data objects that comprise the value stream remain constant. Therefore, it is complementary to both traditional and new methods of service development like agile, SCRUM, or DevOps.

The R2D Value Stream consumes the Conceptual Service produced in the S2P Value Stream and designs the Logical Service, and then through development or sourcing and testing functions, enables the development of the Service Release. A Service Release Blueprint is created based on the Service Release and details the necessary information (configurations, components, deployment patterns) to deliver the service. The service is deployed or fulfilled in the R2F Value Stream once a Service Catalog Entry exists for a specific Service Release Blueprint and further offered and consumed in the R2F Value Stream.

4.2 Key Value Propositions

The key value propositions for adopting the R2D Value Stream are:

- Ensure that the Service Release meets business expectations (quality, utility)
- Make service delivery predictable, even across globally dispersed teams and suppliers, and multiple development methodologies while preserving innovation
- Standardize service development and delivery to the point where re-use of service components is the norm
- Build a culture of collaboration between IT operations and development to improve Service Release success

4.3 Activities

Typical activities include:

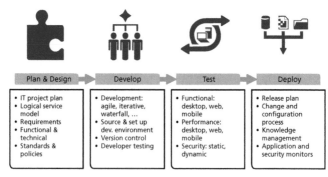

Plan & Design	Develop	Test	Deploy
• IT project plan • Logical service model • Requirements • Functional & technical • Standards & policies	• Development: agile, iterative, waterfall, ... • Source & set up dev. environment • Version control • Developer testing	• Functional: desktop, web, mobile • Performance: desktop, web, mobile • Security: static, dynamic	• Release plan • Change and configuration process • Knowledge management • Application and security monitors

Figure 20: Requirement to Deploy Activities

4.4 Value Stream Diagram

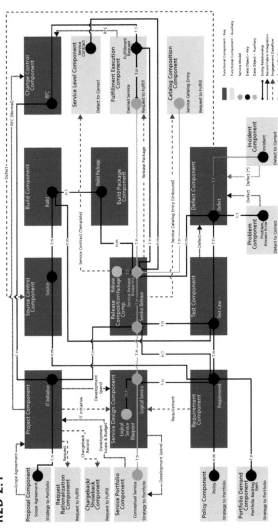

Figure 21: Requirement to Deploy Level 2 Value Stream Diagram

4.5 Project Functional Component

4.5.1 Purpose

The Project functional component coordinates the creation and provides ongoing execution oversight of IT Initiatives aimed at the creation of new or enhancements to existing services. The IT Initiatives are based on the specifications outlined in the Scope Agreement.

The Project functional component will govern, coordinate, influence, and direct initiative execution. It will ensure financial goals and boundary conditions are adhered to and coordinate the acquisition of resources (hardware, software, and people) required to source/create a service in a particular project.

4.5.2 Key Data Objects

The **IT Initiative** data object details the scope of the work to be performed, created from, and associated with the Scope Agreement.

The key attributes are: Id, Name, Status, ServiceReleaseId, RFCId, Budget, ActualSpend, StartDate, EndDate, ScopeAgreementId.

4.5.3 Key Data Object Relationships

Scope Agreement to IT Initiative (1:n): Maintain a linkage between the proposal, which authorized one or more IT Initiatives.

IT Initiative to Service Release (1:n): An IT Initiative will manage the creation of one or more Service Releases required to deliver the IT Initiative.

IT Initiative to Request for Change (RFC) (1:n): An Initiative will be related to one or many RFC records in order to manage all changes resulting from a single work effort (initiative).

4.5.4 Functional Criteria

The Project functional component is the system of record (authoritative source) for all IT Initiatives. IT Initiatives are created based on the specifications outlined in the Scope Agreement; including cost, time, scope, and quality. It maintains the linkage/traceability between Scope Agreements, IT Initiatives, and Service Releases. It manages the status and lifecycle of the IT Initiative, including initiative execution, acquisition of resources, tracking spend, and governance.

It aggregates, tracks, and reports status of resources consumed against a project plan or project burn down, and communicates these to stakeholders via auxiliary functional components such as Resource Management, Supplier Management, and IT Financial Management.

If a Change Control functional component exists, the Project functional component can submit one or more RFCs required for the IT Initiative.

If a Request Rationalization functional component exists, the Project functional component sends a Request when resources are required for the IT Initiative.

If a Proposal functional component exists, the Project functional component is able to receive the Scope Agreement from the Proposal functional component.

If a Service Design functional component exists, the Project functional component can provide IT Initiative information required for service design to the Service Design functional component.

If a Chargeback/Showback functional component exists, the Project functional component receives the subscribed service charges associated with an IT Initiative and sends charge acceptance to the Chargeback/Showback functional component.

If a Service Portfolio functional component exists, the Project functional component receives the development scope and agreement from the Service Portfolio functional component.

4.5.5 Data Architecture Criteria

The Project Functional component manages all aspects of the IT Initiative data object. It allows recursive relationships between IT Initiatives. If a Proposal functional component exists, it associates a Scope Agreement to an IT Initiative. If a Release Composition functional component exists, it associates an IT Initiative to a service. If a Change Control functional component exists, it associates an IT Initiative to an RFC. If the IT Financial Management supporting function exists, it associates an IT Initiative with an IT Budget Item.

Model

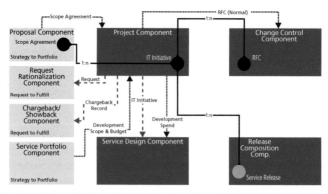

Figure 22: Project Functional Component Level 2 Model

4.6 Requirement Functional Component

4.6.1 Purpose

The Requirement functional component manages requirements through the lifecycle of a service. It collects, refines, scopes, and tracks progress of Requirements even before and after an IT Initiative has concluded. It maintains the traceability of each Requirement to the original source (demand, IT or business standard or policy, and/or requestor) and to appropriate Source and/or Test Cases throughout the service lifecycle.

4.6.2 Key Data Objects
The **Requirement** data object records details of the needs or conditions to meet for a new or altered service.

The key attributes are: Id, Type, Summary, LogicalServiceId, RequirementSource, Owner, ServiceReleaseId.

4.6.3 Key Data Object Relationships
Logical Service Blueprint to Requirement (1:n): One or more Requirements are used to define the required behavior for the Logical Service.

Service Release to Requirement (1:n): The Service Release describes a version of the service which fulfills one or more Requirements.

Requirement to Test Case (1:n): A Requirement is traced to one or more Test Cases to ensure stated needs or conditions have been successfully delivered or met.

Portfolio Backlog Item to Requirement (1:n): A Portfolio Backlog Item is mapped to one or more Requirements that will need to be delivered to successfully fulfill the demand.

Policy to Requirement (n:m): Requirements may be sourced from policies or may reference policies in order to remain in compliance to previously agreed policies for an organization.

Requirement to Source (n:m): Source will fulfill one or many Requirements, and for a given Requirement, there could be multiple Sources created/modified.

4.6.4 Functional Criteria

The Requirement functional component is the system of record (authoritative source) for all Requirements. It manages the lifecycle of the Requirement. It manages the state of a Requirement.

It collects, refines, scopes, and tracks progress of Requirements even before and after an IT Initiative has concluded. It maintains traceability of each Requirement to the original source (demand, IT or business standard or policy, and/or requestor) and to appropriate Source and/or Test Cases throughout the service lifecycle. It derives product or program backlogs, which will ultimately serve as queues for enhancing services. If a Service Design functional component exists, the Requirement functional component manages the data flow to provide Requirement information to the Service Design functional component.

4.6.5 Data Architecture Criteria

The Requirement functional component allows recursive and also hierarchical relationships between Requirements. It associates a requirement to a service.

If a Service Design functional component exists, it associates one or more Requirements to a Logical Service.

If a Policy functional component exists, it associates one or more Requirements to one or more Policies.

If a Portfolio Demand functional component exists, it associates one or more Requirements to a Portfolio Backlog Item.

If a Release Composition functional component exists, it associates one or more Requirements to a Service Release.

If a Source Control functional component exists, it associates one or more Requirements to one or more Source.

If a Test functional component exists, it associates a Requirement to one or more Test Cases.

Model

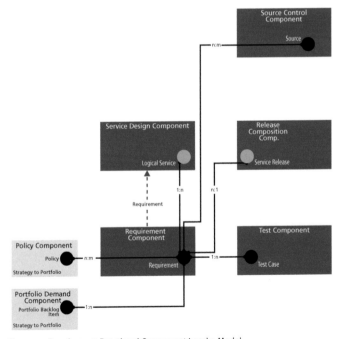

Figure 23: Requirement Functional Component Level 2 Model

4.7 Service Design Functional Component

4.7.1 Purpose

The Service Design functional component identifies the new or existing services required to meet the needs of the Scope Agreement and IT Initiative, including both service systems and service offers. Based on the Conceptual Service and Portfolio Backlog Items, it produces a Logical Service that describes the service structure and behavior considering both the service system and the service offer.

The Service Design functional component creates various architectural artifacts (data flow diagrams, technical schematics, etc.) that comply with the IT Initiative specifications and boundaries. It creates a service design specification document (Logical Service Blueprint). The Logical Service Blueprint identifies the service delivery model (in-source, outsource, etc.), identifies service suppliers to meet the requirements within the chosen delivery model, and enables interaction with IT operations to develop support plan/requirements.

The Service Design functional component ensures that the architecture and Logical Service Blueprint is compliant with all standards and policies, that it meets functional and non-functional requirements, and is consistent with Enterprise Architecture principles and requirements.

4.7.2 Key Data Objects

The **Logical Service** data object represents the bridge between the service interaction and service system.

The key attributes are: Id, Name, Description, ConceptualServiceId, BudgetedSpend, ActualSpend.

The **Logical Service Blueprint** auxiliary data object represents the design of the logical service which details the components and how those components relate to each other.

The key attributes are: Id, Name, Description, Version, LogicalServiceId, ArchitectureDesign.

4.7.3 Key Data Object Relationships

Conceptual Service to Logical Service (1:n): One or more Logical Services represents the logical components which are necessary to provide the expected outcome of the Conceptual Service.

Logical Service to Requirement (1:n): One or more Requirements will be used to define the required behavior from the Logical Service.

Logical Service to Service Release (1:n): A Logical Service can lead to the creation of one or more Service Releases in order to deliver the required service outcomes.

Logical Service to Logical Service Blueprint (1:1): A Logical Service structure and behavior can be detailed by one or more Logical Service Blueprints.

4.7.4 Functional Criteria

The Service Design functional component is the system of record (authoritative source) for all Logical Services. It identifies the new or existing services required to meet the needs of the Scope Agreement and IT Initiative, including both service systems and service offers.

It creates various architectural artifacts (data flow diagrams, technical schematics, etc.) that comply with the IT Initiative specifications and boundaries.

It creates the service design specification document (Logical Service Blueprint) including the service delivery model (in-source, outsource, etc.), supplier identification, and compliance with all standards and policies including security.

It enables interaction with IT operations to develop support plan/
requirements for an IT service, that it is architected to meet the KPIs and
SLAs.

If a Service Portfolio functional component exists, the Service Design
functional component sends development spend information back to the
Conceptual Service in order to manage TCO for the service.

If a Project functional component exists, the Service Design functional
component can receive IT Initiative information, which includes the
scope and some content based on which the service is designed, and also
the development spend to date.

If a Requirement functional component exists, the Service Design
functional component receives Requirement information from the
Requirement functional component used to design the Logical Service
Blueprint and create design specifications.

4.7.5 Data Architecture Criteria

The Service Design functional component manages all aspects of the
Logical Service data object. It associates a Logical Service Blueprint to
a service. It can also associate a Logical Service Blueprint to a Service
Design Package. It tracks the actual spend of a Logical Service.

If a Service Portfolio functional component exists, it associates one or
more Logical Services to a Conceptual Service.

If a Requirement functional component exists, it associates one or more
Requirements to a Logical Service.

If a Release Composition functional component exists, it associates a
Logical Service to one or more Service Releases.

Model

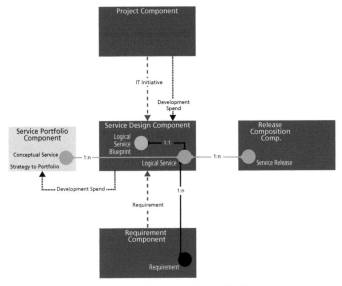

Figure 24: Service Design Functional Component Level 2 Model

4.8 Source Control Functional Component

4.8.1 Purpose

The Source Control functional component manages the development of source code or infrastructure based on the Logical Service, Service Design Package, and IT Initiative priorities. It ensures that the source code meets the design specifications, organizational policies, standards, and non-functional requirements so that the service can be operated successfully and meets customer expectations.

It manages source code images and stores them in a Source data object repository and delivers the Source data object to the Build functional component. It also receives Defects and input from the Defect functional component to enable the development of fixes or documented workarounds.

4.8.2 Key Data Objects

The **Source** data object is the created or purchased solution to meet the requirements for a particular Service Release.

The key attributes are: Id, Version, RequirementId.

 Source does not always equal "source code". Consider all use-cases such as "source code" for services produced on-premise, to contracts or entitlements for services simply subscribed to, to the purchase and implementation of a Commercial Off-The-Shelf (COTS) application.

4.8.3 Key Data Object Relationships

Source to Requirement (n:m): Source will fulfill one or many Requirements, and for a given Requirement, there could be multiple Sources created/modified.

Source to Build (1:n): Source can be built multiple times to create several Build versions.

4.8.4 Functional Criteria

The Source Control functional component is the system of record (authoritative source) for all Source. It manages the lifecycle of the Source, including development, fulfillment of design specifications, adherence to policies and non-functional requirements, testing and defect resolution, and security compliance. It manages source code images and stores them as Source.

If a Defect functional component exists, the Source Control functional component can receive Defect information so Defects can be fixed in future versions of that Source.

4.8.5 Data Architecture Criteria

The Source Control functional component manages all aspects of the Source data object. It allows recursive and also hierarchical relationships between Sources.

If a Requirement functional component exists, it associates one or many Requirements to one or many Sources.

If a Build functional component exists, the Source Control functional component associates one or more Builds to the Source.

Model

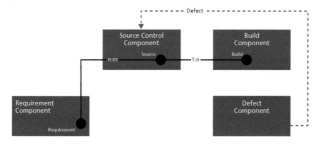

Figure 25: Source Control Functional Component Level 2 Model

4.9 Build Functional Component

4.9.1 Purpose

The Build functional component receives the Source data object from the Source Control functional component and manages the creation, implementation, automation, and security and storage of all Builds. It manages Builds and versioning in a Definitive Media Library (DML).

It automates the Build process through automated Build storage procedures and automated compilation techniques and tools. It also runs dynamic application security testing.

4.9.2 Key Data Objects

The **Build** data object is created from Source and versioned.

The key attributes are: Id, Version, SourceId, TestCaseId, BuildPackageId.

4.9.3 Key Data Object Relationships

Source to Build (1:n): Source can be built multiple times to create several Build versions.

Build to Test Case (n:m): One or many Builds can be related to one or many Test Cases used as part of the Build creation.

Build Package to Build (1:n): A Build Package is comprised of one or many Builds.

4.9.4 Functional Criteria

The Build functional component is the system of record (authoritative source) for all Builds. It manages the lifecycle of the Build including creation, implementation, automation, security, and storage. It manages the Build process to support the Build schedule and Build frequency requirements.

It includes the development of automated Build storage procedures and automated compilation techniques and tools. It monitors and reports on the results of each integration Build.

4.9.5 Data Architecture Criteria

The Build functional component manages all aspects of the Build data object. It manages the version of each individual Build.

If a Source Control functional component exists, it associates Source to one or many Builds.

If a Build Package functional component exists, it associates one or many Builds to a Build Package.

If a Test functional component exists, it associates one or many Builds to one or many Test Cases.

Model

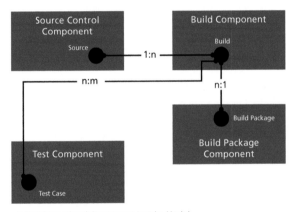

Figure 26: Build Functional Component Level 2 Model

4.10 Build Package Functional Component

4.10.1 Purpose

Creation of a deployable package made up of one or many Builds. Manage the Build Packages and relationships to the Service Release Blueprints.

4.10.2 Key Data Objects

The **Build Package** data object is a compilation of one or many Builds in a deployable package.

The key attributes are: Id, Name.

4.10.3 Key Data Object Relationships

Build Package to Build (1:n): The Build Package is comprised of one or more Builds.

Build Package to Service Release Blueprint (n:m): Multiple Build Packages, which represent the deployable content of the service components, can be deployed using the instructions in the Service Release Blueprints.

4.10.4 Functional Criteria

The Build Package functional component is the system of record (authoritative source) for all Build Packages. It creates a deployable package made up of one or more Builds. It manages the Build Packages and relationships to the Service Release Blueprints.

4.10.5 Data Architecture Criteria

The Build Package functional component manages all aspects of the Build Package data object.

If a Release Composition functional component exists, it associates one or more Build Packages to one or more Service Release Blueprints.

If a Build functional component exists, it associates a Build Package to one or more Builds.

Model

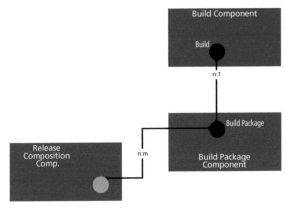

Figure 27: Build Package Functional Component Level 2 Model

4.11 Release Composition Functional Component

4.11.1 Purpose

The Release Composition functional component creates the Release Package, Service Release Blueprints, and overall Service Release for developing and delivering new or changed services to the R2F Value Stream Fulfillment Execution functional component to facilitate a smooth transition to IT operations.

It manages the release artifacts within the Release Package by centralizing all elements of the Service Release Blueprint from the various functional components and begins the creation of monitors, batch processing, backup/restore, etc. for the service, to ensure supportability as part of IT operations enablement.

4.11.2 Key Data Objects

The **Service Release** (data object) represents a planned release of a version of the service system.

The key attributes are: Id, Name, Status, Version, LogicalServiceId, ITInitiativeId.

The **Service Release Blueprint** (data object) provides the planned design/configuration of the components of the service system.

The key attributes are: Id, Name, Description, ServiceReleaseId, BuildPackageId, DefectID, DeploymentModel.

4.11.3 Key Data Object Relationships
The Service Release data object:

Logical Service Blueprint to Service Release (1:n): A Logical Service Blueprint can lead to the creation of one or more Service Releases in order to deliver the required service.

IT Initiative to Service Release (1:n): An IT Initiative will manage the creation of one or more Service Releases defined to deliver the content of the IT Initiative.

Service Release to Service Release Blueprint (1:n): A Service Release can be released to different environments based on different Service Release Blueprints.

Service Release to Requirement (1:n): The Service Release describes a version of the service which fulfills one or more Requirements.

Service Release to Test Case (1:n): A Service Release can be validated by one or many Test Cases.

The Service Release Blueprint data object:

Service Release to Service Release Blueprint (1:n): A Service Release can be released to different environments based on different Service Release Blueprints.

Service Release Blueprint to Build Package (n:m): Multiple Build Packages, which represent the deployable content of the service components, can be deployed using the instructions contained in the Service Release Blueprints.

Service Release Blueprint to Desired Service (1:n): One Service Release Blueprint can be translated to one or more Desired Service(s).

Service Release Blueprint to Fulfillment Request (1:n): One Service Release Blueprint is used for service instantiation by one or many Fulfillment Requests.

Service Release Blueprint to Service Contract (n:m): One or more Service Release Blueprints contain the template of one or more Service Contracts.

Service Catalog Entry to Service Release Blueprint (1:n): Each Service Catalog Entry is created based on definitions of a Service Release Blueprint.

Service Release Blueprint to Defect (n:m): One or more Service Release Blueprints can contain one or more Defects in the form of Problems/Known Errors.

4.11.4 Functional Criteria
The Release Composition functional component is the system of record (authoritative source) for all Service Releases, Service Release Blueprints, and Release Packages.

Model

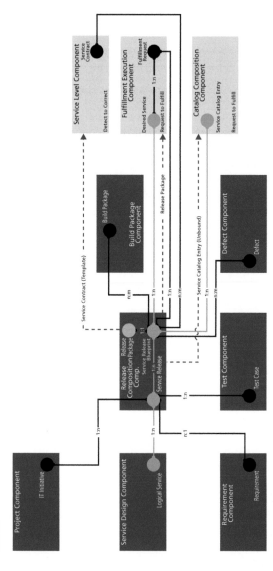

Figure 28: Release Composition Functional Component Level 2 Model

If a Service Level functional component exists, the Release Composition functional component can provide service contract information for creating a Service Contract.

If a Fulfillment Execution functional component exists, the Release Composition functional component can provide information required for service instantiation.

If a Catalog Composition functional component exists, the Release Composition functional component can provide information required for creating a Service Catalog Entry.

4.11.5 Data Architecture Criteria

The Release Composition functional component manages all aspects of the Service Release, Service Release Blueprint, and Release Package data objects. It associates a Service Release to one or more Service Release Blueprints, and associates a Service Release Blueprint to a Release Package.

If a Project functional component exists, it associates one or more Service Releases to an IT Initiative.

If a Service Design functional component exists, it associates one or more Service Releases to a Logical Service.

If a Requirement functional component exists, it associates a Service Release to one or more Requirements.

If a Test functional component exists, it associates a Service Release to one or more Test Cases.

If a Build Package functional component exists, it associates one or more Service Release Blueprints to one or more Build Packages.

If a Fulfillment Execution functional component exists, it associates a Service Release Blueprint to one or more Desired Services, and one or more Fulfillment Requests.

If a Service Level functional component exists, it associates one or more Service Release Blueprints to one or more Service Contracts.

If a Catalog Composition functional component exists, it associates a Service Release Blueprint to one or more Service Catalog Entries.

If a Defect functional component exists, it associates one or more Service Release Blueprints to one or more Defects.

4.12 Test Functional Component

4.12.1 Purpose

The Test functional component plans and executes tests that ensure the IT service will support the customer's requirements at the agreed service levels. It prepares the test environment, plans and designs tests, and executes all functional and non-functional tests including performance and stress testing.

It creates Defect data objects that are consumed by the Defect functional component. It provides test execution reports for the tested Requirements and ensures that the operations tooling works as expected (monitors, etc.).

4.12.2 Key Data Objects

The **Test Case** data object is used to validate that the Service Release is fit-for-purpose.

The key attributes are: Id, Name, Description, Status, Result, ServiceReleaseId, RequirementId.

4.12.3 Key Data Object Relationships

Requirement to Test Case (1:n): A Requirement is associated to one or more Test Cases that validates this Requirement.

Service Release to Test Case (1:n): A Service Release is associated to one or more Test Cases which are executed as part of this Service Release.

Test Case to Build (n:m): One or more Test Cases can be associated with one or more Builds that uses this Test Case as part of the Build creation.

Test Case to Defect (1:n): One Test Case can be associated to one or more Defects that are reported as a result of this test.

4.12.4 Functional Criteria

The Test functional component is the system of record (authoritative source) for all Test Cases. It manages the lifecycle of the Test Case. It plans, designs, and executes tests that ensure the service will support the customer's requirements. It ensures test automation re-use and test scripts. It prepares test environments and manages test data. It executes tests including functionality tests, usability tests, acceptance tests, risk-based security test, performance test, and stress tests. It provides test execution reports. It passes Defects identified during test execution to the Defect functional component.

4.12.5 Data Architecture Criteria

The Test functional component manages all aspects of the Test Case data object. It allows recursive relationships between Test Cases.

If a Requirement functional component exists, it associates a Requirement to one or more Test Cases that validates this Requirement.

If a Build functional component exists, it associates one or more Test Cases to one or more Builds.

If a Defect functional component exists, it associates a Test Case to one or more Defects.

Model

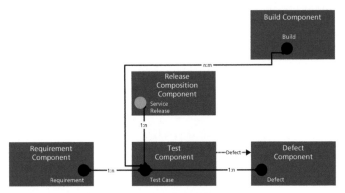

Figure 29: Test Functional Component Level 2 Model

4.13 Defect Functional Component

4.13.1 Purpose
The Defect functional component keeps track of all Defects by registering Defects of all types (including security-related Defects). It analyzes Defects and finds resolutions. It also associates Defects with Requirements.

It documents issues that should be communicated to the Release Composition functional component. It decides on target release and reports Defect status. It also converts Defects not resolved to Known Errors for Problem Management.

4.13.2 Key Data Objects
The **Defect** data object is an issue with the Service Release Blueprint which should be remediated to fulfill the associated Requirements.

The key attributes are: Id, Title, Description, Status, TestCaseId.

4.13.3 Key Data Object Relationships
Test Case to Defect (1:n): One Test Case can be associated to one or more Defects that results from the test.

Defect to Service Release Blueprint (n:m): One or more Service Release Blueprints are associated to one or more Defects which are included in the Release Package as Problems/Known Errors.

Known Error to Defect (1:1): A Known Error may be the source for submitting a new Defect.

Incident to Defect (1:1): A current practice that replaces the Known Error path when that one does not exist. An Incident may be the source for submitting a new Defect.

4.13.4 Functional Criteria
The Defect functional component is the system of record (authoritative source) for all Defects. It manages the lifecycle of the Defect, including its origin, status, importance, and relation to Requirements and Known Errors. It manages relevant details about the Defect, such as description, severity, application version, related requirement, and target release.

4.13.5 Data Architecture Criteria
The Defect functional component manages all aspects of the Defect data object.

If a Release Composition functional component exists, it associates one or more Defects to one or more Service Release Blueprints.

If a Test functional component exists, it associates one or more Defects to a Test Case.

If a Problem functional component exists, it associates a Defect to a Known Error.

Model

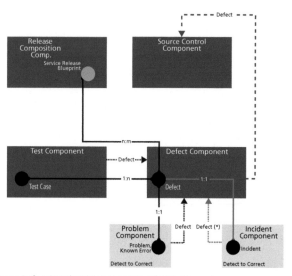

Figure 30: Defect Functional Component Level 2 Model

Chapter 5
The R2F Value Stream

This chapter describes the Request to Fulfill (R2F) Value Stream.

5.1 Overview

The Request to Fulfill (R2F) Value Stream:

- Helps your IT organization transition to a service broker model
- Presents a single catalog with items from multiple supplier catalogs
- Manages and measures fulfillments across multiple suppliers
- Efficiently manages subscriptions and total cost of service
- Tracks actual usage of subscribed IT services

The Request to Fulfill (R2F) Value Stream is a framework connecting the various consumers (business users, IT practitioners, or end customers) with goods and services that are used to satisfy productivity and innovation needs. The R2F Value Stream places emphasis on time-to-value, repeatability, and consistency for consumers looking to request and obtain services from IT. The R2F Value Stream helps IT optimize both service consumption and fulfillment experiences for users by delineating functions for an Offer Catalog and Catalog Composition. The R2F Value Stream framework provides a single consumption experience to consumers for seamless subscription to both internal and external services, as well as managing subscriptions and routing fulfillments to different service providers using the R2F Value Stream framework.

The R2F Value Stream plays an important role in helping IT organizations transition to a service broker model. Enterprise customers have been using external suppliers for goods and services for many years. The IT multi-sourcing environment will accelerate as companies adopt cloud computing offerings like Infrastructure as a Service (IaaS), Platform as a Service (PaaS), and Software as a Service (SaaS).

The R2F Value Stream also enables effective chargeback and service costing mechanisms, a key requirement in a multi-sourcing environment.

5.2 Key Value Propositions

The key value propositions for adopting the R2F Value Stream are:

- Provide a portal and catalog blueprint for facilitating a service consumption experience that allows consumers to easily find and subscribe to services through self-service, regardless of sourcing approach
- Establish the model for moving from traditional IT request management to service brokerage
- Increase fulfillment efficiency through standard change deployment and automation
- Leverage the common Service Model to reduce custom service request fulfillments and design automated fulfillments
- Facilitate a holistic view and traceability across service subscription, service usage, and service chargeback to improve IT Financial Management

5.3 Activities

Typical activities include:

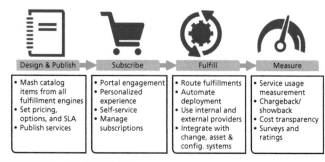

Figure 31: Request to Fulfill Activities

5.4 Value Stream Diagram

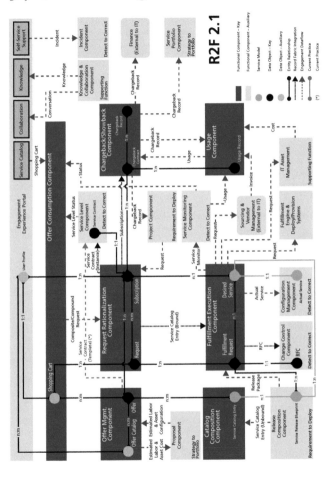

Figure 32: Request to Fulfill Level 2 Value Stream Diagram

5.5 Engagement Experience Portal

 The Engagement Experience Portal is a Secondary Functional Component; refer to *Functional Component* within Section 2.2.3.

5.5.1 Purpose

The Engagement Experience Portal facilitates service consumption by connecting any potential consumer with the right information, goods, services, or capability at the right time through a single experience, taking into account the consumer profile. It is based on system of engagement design patterns where consumers access different functional components through a common user experience.

Through the Engagement Experience Portal, the consumer has access to self-service support functionalities like community and collaboration, knowledge associated with services, information about consumed services, and service status.

5.5.2 Key Data Objects

The **User Profile** data object contains personal data associated with a specific user and the explicit digital representation of a person's identity.

The key attributes are: Id, Name, Role.

5.5.3 Key Data Object Relationships

User Profile to Offer Catalog (n:m): Presents a personalized list of offers from the catalog depending on the consumer profile.

User Profile to Shopping Cart (1:1): Establishes the link between the catalog items, which are ordered, and the consumer and helps to identify the authorized person where an approval is required.

Model

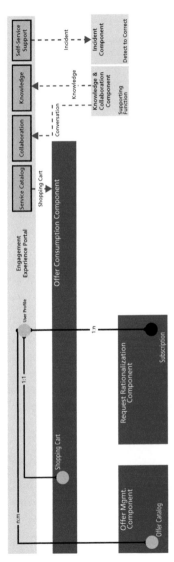

Figure 33: Engagement Experience Portal Level 2 Model

User Profile to Subscription (1:n): Creates a link between the user and a subscription for every service where a Subscription is required.

5.5.4 Functional Criteria

The Engagement Experience Portal functional component is available to all users that desire to consume IT services. It exposes various IT functions and capabilities in a single place, unifying the experience. It allows consumers to manage their User Profile (to varying degrees as some attributes may be provider-controlled).

The Engagement Experience Portal also includes the following sub-components:

- The Service Catalog functional sub-component enables consumers to engage with and consume services through the Offer Consumption functional component
- The Collaboration functional sub-component provides the user front end for an enterprise collaboration experience, such as a chat capability
- The Knowledge functional sub-component provides the interface for users to search and read knowledge data objects of all types and sources
- The Self-Service Support functional sub-component provides service consumers with a way to address more of their IT-related issues, as well as receive information regarding their existing records without necessarily engaging IT providers; it enables users to create new support tickets, view and update their existing support tickets, and access the Knowledge data objects

5.6 Offer Consumption Functional Component

5.6.1 Purpose

The Offer Consumption functional component presents consumable offers derived from Service Catalog Entries with associated descriptions, pictures, prices, and purchasing options to prospective consumers. It facilitates consumption/management of and payment for IT services rendered. It enables consumers to manage their subscriptions.

5.6.2 Key Data Objects

The **Shopping Cart** data object contains the IT services that the user wants to order; the object only exists during the actual shopping session.

The key attributes are: Id, UserId, ApproverId, Status. And for every item in the Shopping Cart: LineItem, OfferId, RequestId.

5.6.3 Key Data Object Relationships

Shopping Cart to User Profile (1:1): Relates the contents of the Shopping Cart to a specific user, who is actually ordering the services.

Shopping Cart to Offer (n:m): Presents those items available to the end-user from the existing Offers.

Shopping Cart to Request (1:n): Establishes the link between the Shopping Cart and the Requests necessary to fulfill the services ordered in the shopping experience.

5.6.4 Functional Criteria

The Offer Consumption functional component provides information on items users need to order from existing offers and shall provide all necessary information to guarantee the fulfillment. It also provides information on the existing Subscription, and its specific service consumption, to enable the user to change/cancel existing Subscriptions. It allows consumers to order multiple offers in one transaction and enables consumers to order services on behalf of other consumers.

If the Service Level functional component exists, the Offer Consumption functional component exposes information on the Service Level status for the services to which the user subscribed.

Model

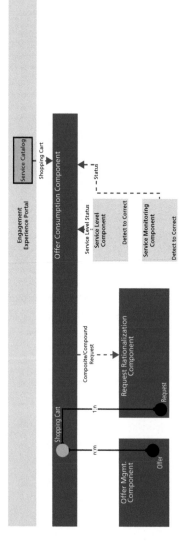

Figure 34: Offer Consumption Functional Component Level 2 Model

5.7 Offer Management Functional Component

5.7.1 Purpose
The Offer Management functional component aggregates all Catalog Composition items and external supplier catalogs into consumable offers. It builds and publishes the various offerings into Offer Catalogs for various populations. It also fulfills each Offer through numerous underlying Catalog Compositions.

5.7.2 Key Data Objects
The **Offer data** object defines how a Service Catalog Entry will be instantiated and under what terms and conditions – price, deployment, approval, workflow, service level (contract), etc.

The key attributes are: Id, CatalogId, Name, StartDate, ExpiryDate, Status, Price, ReqValue, ServiceId.

The **Offer Catalog** auxiliary data object is a set or collection of Offers that are grouped together as something that can be consumed by certain consumers or consumer groups.

The key attributes are: Id, Name, Roles.

5.7.3 Key Data Object Relationships
The Offer data object:

Offer to Service Catalog Entry (n:m): Ensures all required information is captured for the fulfillment (deployment/delivery) of the service.

Offer to Shopping Cart (n:m): Each Offer may appear in multiple Shopping Carts and each Shopping Cart may include multiple Offers.

The Offer Catalog data object:

Offer Catalog to Offer (n:m): Defines the collection of Offers that comprise each Offer Catalog.

Offer Catalog to User Profile (n:m): Defines which users can access/consume each Offer Catalog.

5.7.4 Functional Criteria

The Offer Management functional component provides all of the offers available to consumers to the Offer Consumption functional component. It allows to group services from multiple service providers (internal and external) into a single offer. It may create the Service Contract template and provide information to the Service Level functional component.

It builds and publishes the various Offers into Offer Catalogs for various populations to consume and determine prices, and valid options that consumers can select.

It enables Offers to be grouped into an Offer Catalog to expose them as a collection of consumable items for a given group of consumers.

It fulfills each Offer through numerous underlying Catalog Compositions as determined by the Offer Management functional component.

It may also send labor and asset cost estimates to the Proposal functional component if a Proposal functional component exists. It may receive estimation about labor and asset configuration from the Proposal functional component if a Proposal functional component exists.

Model

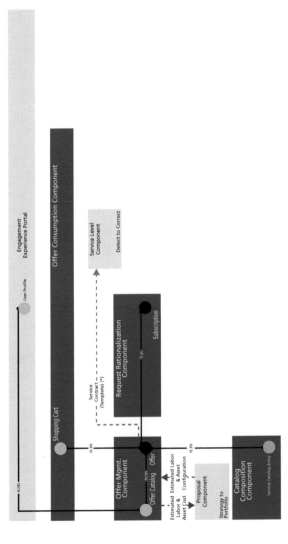

Figure 35: Offer Management Functional Component Level 2 Model

5.8 Catalog Composition Functional Component

5.8.1 Purpose
The Catalog Composition functional component creates, updates, and publishes Service Catalog Entries including all their dependencies necessary to be presented as an Offer in the Offer Management functional component. Service Catalog Entries are created from the Service Release Blueprint in the Release Composition functional component.

5.8.2 Key Data Objects
The **Service Catalog Entry** data object is an authoritative source for the consolidated set of technical capabilities and specific options available from a service system, which can be delivered by the service provider. It serves as the bridge between the service system and the service offer.

The key attributes are: ID, Name, ReqValue.

5.8.3 Key Data Object Relationships
Service Catalog Entry to Service Release Blueprint (n:1): Ensures all catalog entries relate to the specific service definitions used for fulfillment.

Service Catalog Entry to Offer (n:m): Ensures all information needed is captured during the order phase.

5.8.4 Functional Criteria
The Catalog Composition functional component manages inter-dependencies within the services.

It creates and publishes the Service Catalog Entries, including all of their dependencies, at the level at which these can be presented as Offers in the Offer Management functional component.

It creates Service Catalog Entries from the Service Release Blueprint in the Release Composition functional component (R2D Value Stream).

It accurately defines services, as well as their dependencies and details, including the necessary information for the service to be instantiated.

It creates and updates Service Catalog Entries to prepare them for consumption, including configurable options (e.g., pricing, subscription terms, bundles, service level, support conditions, etc.).

Model

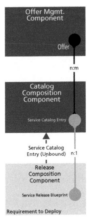

Figure 36: Catalog Composition Functional Component Level 2 Model

5.9 Request Rationalization Functional Component

5.9.1 Purpose
The Request Rationalization functional component rationalizes, breaks down, and routes "clean order" requests (ready for fulfillment) to appropriate Fulfillment Execution engines or providers in order to deliver services to consumers. This may involve breaking down a single order/

request into multiple Fulfillment Requests, and providing these to the Fulfillment Execution functional component. Subscriptions for these services are created (or updated) upon their successful fulfillment.

It ensures appropriate fulfillment-related Subscription information is kept up-to-date, such as approval/rejections, modifications, cancellations, and so on. It also enables the recording of patterns of service consumption that can be used to shape demand for new and/or improved services.

5.9.2 Key Data Objects

The **Request** data object contains all Offers from the Shopping Cart which have been consumed and need to be fulfilled.

The key attributes are: Id, UserId, Status, Date, LatestFulFillDate, ActFulFillDate, SubscriptionId, ServiceId, ReqValue.

The **Subscription** data object represents the rights to access a service that has been provided to a consumer.

The key attributes are: Id, OfferId, UserId, DesireServiceId.

5.9.3 Key Data Object Relationships

The Request data object:

Request to Shopping Cart (n:1): Enables the traceability of Requests to the originating order (in the form of the Shopping Cart).

Request to Subscription (n:m): Enables traceability between the Request and the resulting Subscription.

Request to Fulfillment Request (1:n): Used for tracking fulfillment as well as to navigate between dependent Fulfillment Requests.

The Subscription data object:

Subscription to User Profile (n:1): Enables consumers to manage all of their Subscriptions.

Subscription to Offer (n:1): Provides traceability between the Subscription and the Service Contract (via the Offer).

Subscription to Chargeback Contract (1:n): Facilitates the various chargeback/showback calculations that are dependent on Subscription details such as its contract duration and service status.

Subscription to Desired Service Model (n:1): Enables traceability between the consumer, their Subscription, and the realized service.

5.9.4 Functional Criteria

The Request Rationalization functional component provides information on the fulfillment status, information on Subscription for the associated Chargeback Contract, and information on Request delivery times for SLA measurements.

It breaks down the composite request (described by the Shopping Cart and consumer-selected values) into the individual Requests that need to be fulfilled by the Fulfillment Execution functional component and creates the Subscriptions for these services upon their successful fulfillment. It also sends the bound Service Catalog Entry to the Fulfillment Execution functional component.

It provides Subscription information to the Project functional component for associated Fulfillment Requests.

It ensures appropriate fulfillment-related Subscription information is kept up-to-date, such as approval/rejections, modifications, cancellations, and so on.

Model

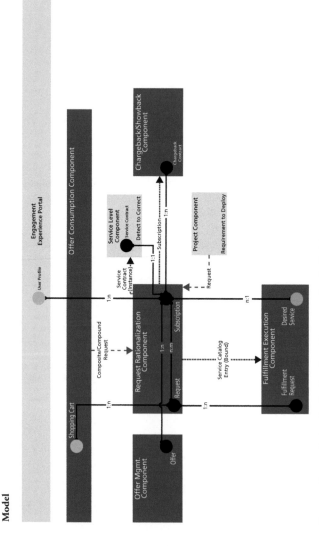

Figure 37: Request Rationalization Functional Component Level 2 Model

It enables the recording of patterns of service consumption that can be used to shape demand for new and/or improved services.

It tracks the fulfillment status and completion notifications from fulfillment channel(s) as received and updates consumers on order status at the Subscription level.

It sends the instances of the Service Contracts to the Service Level functional component if a Service Level functional component exists.

5.10 Fulfillment Execution Functional Component

5.10.1 Purpose

The Fulfillment Execution functional component orchestrates the delivery of the various requests amongst (one or more) fulfillment engines in order to deliver the IT service.

To engage the fulfillers (systems, engaged systems, or external providers that perform actions), the Fulfillment Execution functional component manages a registry of the available fulfillers, takes the bound Service Catalog Entry, and generates both the relevant Fulfillment Requests and the Desired Service data object. It updates the IT asset inventory as they are ordered. It also requests standard changes and updates the Configuration Management functional component (if needed) on delivery of components. It maintains visibility into supplier capacity levels and raises alerts if capacity appears to be insufficient for immediate demand.

The Fulfillment Execution functional component can be used via two paradigms:

- **Consumer-driven** – a consumer request results in a bound Service Catalog Entry which is broken down into the necessary Fulfillment Requests needed to fulfill the originating request

- **Direct access** (without a Service Catalog Entry) – in cases in which there aren't sufficient catalog entries to describe the fulfillment and no entries are planned to be created, the Release Composition functional component (R2D Value Stream) engages and provides enough information to the Fulfillment Execution functional component in order to create the Fulfillment Request(s) necessary to perform the actions needed

5.10.2 Key Data Objects

The **Fulfillment Request** data object describes all fulfillment aspects of an IT service.

The key attributes are: Id, RequestId, DesiredServiceId, RFCId, Status.

The **Desired Service** data object is the specification of an instance of a service as required to meet the fulfillment requirements detailed in the consumer order (Request) and supported by a single Service Release Blueprint.

The key attributes are: Id, SubscriptionId, ServiceReleaseBlueprintId.

5.10.3 Key Data Object Relationships

The Fulfillment Request data object:

Fulfillment Request to Request (n:1): Informs on Fulfillment Request status.

Fulfillment Request to Service Release Blueprint (n:1): Allows the Service Release Blueprint to supply the Fulfillment Request with information needed to instantiate the service.

Fulfillment Request to Desired Service (n:1): Acquires relevant information.

Fulfillment Request to RFC (1:1): Enables, if applicable, the RFC created to be linked to the originating Request.

The Desired Service data object:

Desired Service to Subscription (n:1): Creates the traceability from service to Subscription.

Desired Service to Service Release Blueprint (n:1): Acquires all necessary service information for fulfillment.

Desired Service to Actual Service (1:1): Creates traceability and enables verification of correct deployment/fulfillment.

5.10.4 Functional Criteria

The Fulfillment Execution functional component selects the appropriate fulfillment mechanism, coordinates if multiple fulfillment mechanisms are needed, and manages the dependencies required to fulfill the IT service request. It orchestrates the delivery of the various Requests amongst (one or more) fulfillment engines in order to deliver the IT service. It may engage directly with fulfillment engines, with other systems, or with external providers involved in the fulfillment.

It also provides the Subscription status to the Request Rationalization functional component. It creates one or more Desired Services based on the Service Release Blueprint and associated Subscription for new service deployment Requests. It creates the Actual Services as a copy of the Desired Service within the Configuration Management functional component.

If necessary, the Fulfillment Execution functional component creates an RFC associated with the service instantiation that is created within the Change Control functional component (D2C Value Stream).

Model

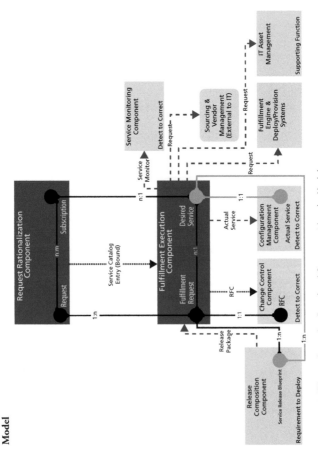

Figure 38: Fulfillment Execution Functional Component Level 2 Model

It can create a new Service Monitor or modify an existing one for the service provided in the Request as part of fulfillment.

It may manage a registry of the available fulfillers to include what each fulfiller does (capabilities) and how to engage each fulfiller (where they are located and how to invoke them).

It may take the bound Service Catalog Entry and generate both the relevant Fulfillment Requests in order to realize/fulfill the originating consumer request and the Desired Service data object which represents the Service Model in its pre-configured or consumer configured state.

It may update the IT asset inventory as they are ordered, and update the Configuration Management functional component on delivery of components.

It maintains visibility into supplier capacity levels and raises alerts if capacity appears to be insufficient for immediate demand.

It can request IT assets necessary for fulfillment (such as licenses). This also enables the tracking of assets being requested or procured and links them with the services that require them.

5.11 Usage Functional Component

5.11.1 Purpose
The Usage functional component tracks and manages actual usage of subscribed IT services and their associated costs.

5.11.2 Key Data Objects
The **Usage Record** data object is the measured use of a particular service or service component.

The key attributes are: Id, ChargebackContractId, UsageDateFrom, UsageDataTo, Units, UnitType.

5.11.3 Key Data Object Relationships

Usage Record to Chargeback Contract (n:1): Every Usage Record for a Subscription is associated with a Chargeback Contract. The Chargeback Contract defines the billing rule and frequency for a service Subscription.

5.11.4 Functional Criteria

The Usage functional component tracks actual Usage of subscribed IT services by gathering IT service Usage metrics, activity, and history for both internal and external sourced IT services associated to an aspect of the Desired Service. It may collect these service Usage metrics from the Service Monitoring functional component (D2C Value Stream). Furthermore, it generates service Usage history and activity reports.

It encrypts sensitive usage information or sets appropriate access controls. It may also provide usage information to the Chargeback Contract component enabling usage-based showback or chargeback.

It collects cost associated with sub-services if a service is further decomposed as well as costs of assets partaking in the delivery of the service. This will be cost reported as Chargeback Records on the sub-services and will be reported as Usage back-up to the next level in the service composition.

It collects Usage information from vendor invoices that represent resources used by the service.

Model

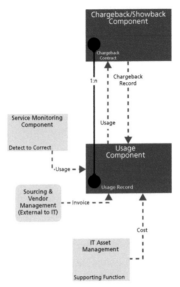

Figure 39: Usage Functional Component Level 2 Model

5.12 Chargeback/Showback Functional Component

5.12.1 Purpose
The Chargeback/Showback functional component provides chargeback or showback for services based on Subscription, Service Contract, and/or Usage information.

5.12.2 Key Data Objects
The **Chargeback Contract** data object details the financial obligations between the service consumer and provider(s).

The key attributes are: Id, SubscriptionId, BillingRule, BillingFrequency, Status.

The **Chargeback Record** data object represents the actual charge to the subscriber based on the Usage of subscribed services in a given time period.

The key attributes are: ChargebackContractId, ChargebackDateFrom, ChargebackDataTo, SubscriptionId, BillAmount, BillStatus.

5.12.3 Key Data Object Relationships

Chargeback Contract to Subscription (n:1): Provides the traceability between the service rendered and the expected charges for those services.

Chargeback Contract to Chargeback Record (1:n): Multiple billing records can be generated for a single Chargeback Contract as the Chargeback Record will be generated for each billing period.

5.12.4 Functional Criteria

The Chargeback/Showback functional component calculates the chargeback/showback of consuming/subscribing to a service to the subscriber. It takes actual Usage into consideration when calculating the price of consuming a service.

It consolidates the charges from all subscribed services once Usage is collected for the given billing period.

It may send the consolidated service charges to the Project functional component if a Project functional component exists.

It sends the subscribed service charges to the Service Portfolio functional component for an Actual Service if a Service Portfolio functional component exists.

It sends a Chargeback Record for approval and internal reconciliation request to the Finance function if a Finance function (external to IT) exists.

Model

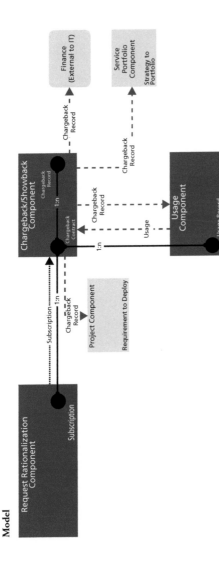

Figure 40: Chargeback/Showback Functional Component Level 2 Model

5.13 Knowledge & Collaboration Supporting Function

5.13.1 Purpose
The Knowledge & Collaboration supporting function provides knowledge and conversations that help to address the needs of IT service consumers. It includes articles, conversations from users, webinars, videos, training materials, etc. It encourages users and IT staff to contribute to knowledge in order to reduce the number of requests for information/knowledge that arrive at the IT service desk.

5.13.2 Key Data Objects
The **Knowledge** data object is structured and unstructured Knowledge from the Knowledge & Collaboration component.

The key attributes are: Id, AuthorId, ActualServiceId, ProblemId, Status, PublishDate, ExpiryDate, Title, Body.

The **Conversation** data object gathers user conversations from the Knowledge & Collaboration component.

The key attributes are: UserId, KnowledgeId, Body.

5.13.3 Key Data Object Relationships
Knowledge to Problem (n:m): Links a Problem to the Knowledge involved.

Knowledge to Conversation (n:m): Links a Conversation to the Knowledge involved.

5.13.4 Functional Criteria
The Knowledge & Collaboration component enables SMEs to submit and/or approve Knowledge data objects. It provides functionality to enable the IT service consumers and IT staff to rank Knowledge data objects and Conversations. It also provides functionality to enable

Model

Figure 41: Knowledge & Collaboration Supporting Function Level 2 Model

IT service consumers to participate in Conversations relating to the
IT services they consume. Furthermore, it can aggregate multiple
Knowledge sources, including third-party Knowledge.

It may include structured IT/supplier produced articles, or unstructured
Conversations from business/IT users, webinars, videos, training
materials, etc. which are searchable by the IT service consumers.

It provides easy access to information/knowledge through the
Engagement Experience Portal using different methods such as natural
language queries, keyword search capabilities, trending topics, etc.

It increases the contribution to Knowledge by providing all users
with the ability to generate new content, either through informal
Conversations, or by more formal submissions of Knowledge.

IT staff may participate in Conversations related to IT services that they
plan, develop, or operate.

Chapter 6
The D2C Value Stream

This chapter describes the Detect to Correct (D2C) Value Stream.

6.1 Overview
The Detect to Correct (D2C) Value Stream:
- Brings together IT service operations to enhance results and efficiency
- Enables end-to-end visibility using a shared configuration model
- Identifies issues before they affect users
- Reduces the MTTR

The Detect to Correct (D2C) Value Stream provides a framework for integrating the monitoring, management, remediation, and other operational aspects associated with realized services and/or those under construction. It also provides a comprehensive overview of the business of IT operations and the services these teams deliver. Anchored by the Service Model, the D2C Value Stream delivers new levels of insight which help improve understanding of the inter-dependencies among the various operational domains; including Event, Incident, Problem, Change Control, and Configuration Management. It also provides the business context for operational requests and new requirements. The D2C Value Stream is designed to accommodate a variety of sourcing methodologies across services, technologies, and functions. This value stream understands the inter-relationships and inter-dependencies required to fix operational issues. It supports IT business objectives of greater agility, improved uptime, and lower cost per service.

The D2C Value Stream provides a framework for bringing IT service operations functions together to enhance IT results and efficiencies. Data in each operation's domain is generally not shared with other domains because they do not understand which key data objects to share and do not have a common language for sharing. When projects are created to solve this, it is often too difficult and cumbersome to finish or there is an internal technology or organization shift that invalidates the result.

The D2C Value Stream defines the functional components and the data that needs to flow between components that enhance a business and service-oriented approach to maintenance and facilitates data flow to the other value streams.

6.2 Key Value Propositions

The key value propositions for adopting the D2C Value Stream are:
- Timely identification and prioritization of an issue
- Improved data sharing to accelerate ability to understand the business impact
- Automation both within domains and across domains
- Ensuring an operating model, capabilities, and processes that can handle the complexity of service delivery across multiple internal and external domains
- Effective linkage of Events to Incidents to Problems to Defects in the R2D Value Stream

6.3 Activities

Typical activities include:

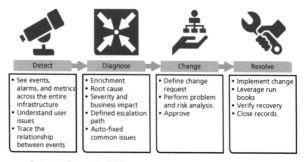

Figure 42: Detect to Correct Activities

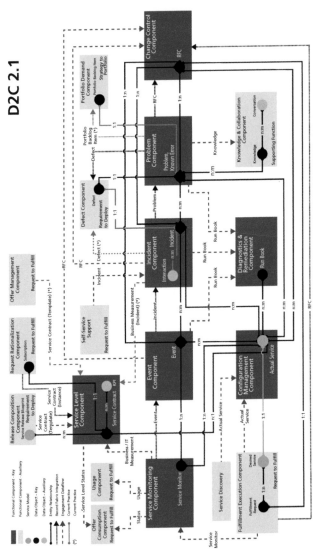

Figure 43: Detect to Correct Level 2 Value Stream Diagram

6.4 Service Monitoring Functional Component

6.4.1 Purpose
The Service Monitoring function component is in charge of creating, running, and managing monitors, which measure all aspects/layers of a service such as infrastructure (system and network), application, and security.

6.4.2 Key Data Objects
The **Service Monitor** data object performs the operational measurement aspects of a CI or an IT service.

The key attributes are: Id, Name, Description, Type, MeasurementDefinitions, LastRunTime, LastRunStatus, ActualServiceId.

6.4.3 Key Data Object Relationships
Service Monitor to Event (1:n): Enables traceability from the Events that are created to the Service Monitor from which they originated.

Service Monitor to Actual Service (1:n): Identifies the Actual Service being monitored.

6.4.4 Functional Criteria
The Service Monitoring functional component is the system of record for all Service Monitors. It performs monitoring of all aspects of an IT service, stores all the results of the measurement being done, and calculates results of compound Service Monitors. It manages the lifecycle of the Service Monitor. It creates, runs, and manages monitors that measure all aspects/layers of a service.

6.4.5 Data Architecture Criteria
The Service Monitoring functional component initiates the creation of an Event or alert that is passed to the Event functional component.

It can provide service monitoring status to the Offer Consumption functional component, service usage measurements to the Usage functional component, and business/IT measurements to the Service Level component.

It may receive Service Monitor definitions from the Fulfillment Execution functional component.

Model

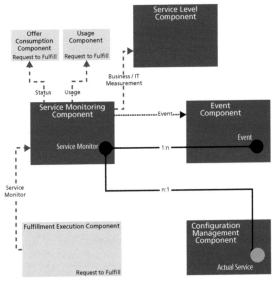

Figure 44: Service Monitoring Functional Component Level 2 Model

6.5 Event Functional Component

6.5.1 Purpose
The Event functional component manages Events through the Event lifecycle for events that occur on any IT service.

6.5.2 Key Data Objects

The **Event** data object represents an alert/notification signifying a change of state of a monitored CI.

The key attributes are: Id, Name, Category, Type, Status, StatusTime, Severity, ThresholdDefinitions, AssignedTo, IsCorrelated, ActualServiceId.

6.5.3 Key Data Object Relationships

Event to Incident (n:m): Enables the connection between the Incidents and Events.

Event to RFC (1:n): Associates an Event for the RFC processing.

Event to Actual Service (n:m): Identifies Actual Service(s) associated with the Event(s).

Service Monitor to Event (1:n): Enables traceability from the Events that are created to the Service Monitor from which they originated.

6.5.4 Functional Criteria

The Event functional component is the system of record for all Events. It manages the state and lifecycle of the Events, and the correlation between Events. It categorizes Event data, and forwards Events categorized as Incidents to the Incident functional component.

It may initiate a change request (RFC) based on Event data to the Change Control functional component. It may send Events for diagnostics and remediation processing to the Diagnostics & Remediation functional component.

6.5.5 Data Architecture Criteria

The Event functional component creates an association between the Event data object and the related Actual Service(s).

Model

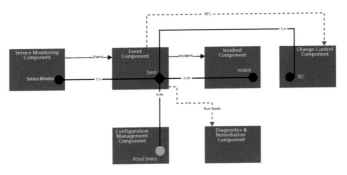

Figure 45: Event Functional Component Level 2 Model

6.6 Incident Functional Component

6.6.1 Purpose

The Incident functional component facilitates normal service operations restoration as quickly as possible and minimizes the impact on business operations, thus optimizing service quality and availability.

An Incident is defined as an unplanned interruption to an IT service or reduction in the quality of an IT service as defined within the Service Contract related to the IT service.

An Interaction is a record of any end-user contact with the service desk agent.

6.6.2 Key Data Objects

The **Incident** data object hosts and manages Incident data.

The key attributes are: Id, Category, SubCategory, Status, StatusTime, Severity, Priority, Title, Description, AssignedTo, ActualServiceId.

The **Interaction** auxiliary data object hosts the record of an end-user's contact with the service desk.

The key attribute is: Id.

6.6.3 Key Data Object Relationships

Incident to Problem, Known Error (n:m): Establishes connection between the Incidents that are converted to Problems.

Incident to RFC (1:n): Connects RFCs to the Incidents from which they originated.

Incident to Defect (1:1): Determines there is a need for an emergency fix from development.

Incident to Actual Service (n:m): Identifies Actual Service(s) to which the Incident is associated and usually the main subject of.

Event to Incident (n:m): Enables the connection between the Incidents and Events.

6.6.4 Functional Criteria

The Incident functional component is the system of record for all Incidents. It manages the state escalation paths and general lifecycle of the Incident. It allows an Incident to be initiated from an Event, and creates an Incident when an Interaction cannot be associated with an existing Incident because it requires additional clarification, diagnostics, or support actions.

6.6.5 Data Architecture Criteria

The Incident functional component creates an association between the Incident data object and the related Actual Service(s). It may initiate the creation of a Defect to the Defect functional component when Incident diagnostics determines that an emergency fix is required from

Model

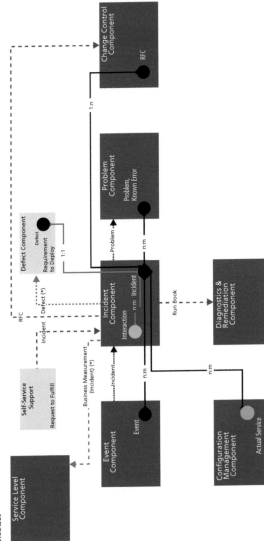

Figure 46: Incident Functional Component Level 2 Model

development for resolution. It can trigger the execution of a Run Book (either automated or manual) to provide diagnostic information or remediation steps.

It may create a Problem record to the Problem functional component when the Incident is severe, requires further deep investigation, or is repeating. It can trigger the creation of an RFC to the Change Control functional component in order to implement a fix to the Incident fault. It can allow the initiation of an Interaction or an Incident to the Self-Service Support functional component. It can provide business measurements of Incident data to the Service Level functional component.

6.7 Problem Functional Component

6.7.1 Purpose
The Problem functional component is responsible for managing the lifecycle of all Problems. The objectives of the Problem functional component are to solve severe/repeating Incidents, prevent Incidents from happening, and minimize the impact of Incidents that cannot be prevented.

6.7.2 Key Data Objects
The **Problem, Known Error** data object defines the Problem or Known Error and manages the Problem and Known Error lifecycle.

The key attributes are: Id, Category, SubCategory, Status, StatusTime, Title, Description, AssignedTo, ActualServiceId.

6.7.3 Key Data Object Relationships
Problem, Known Error to RFC (1:n): Enables the relation of an RFC record that is created when problem resolution requires a change.

Problem, Known Error to Portfolio Backlog Item (1:1): Ensures a Portfolio Backlog Item is created for Problems requiring a future fundamental/big fix/enhancement to the IT service.

Problem, Known Error to Defect (1:1): Enables the creation of Defects when emergency/specific fixes require development.

Incident to Problem, Known Error (n:m): Establishes connection between the Incidents that are converted to Problems.

Problem, Known Error to Actual Service (n:m): Identifies Actual Service(s) to which the Problem is associated.

Problem, Known Error to Knowledge (n:m): Creates a relationship between the Knowledge data object and the Problem from which it originated.

6.7.4 Functional Criteria

The Problem functional component is the system of record for all Problem records. It manages the state and lifecycle of the Problem, and creates Known Error data object instances from unsolved Problems.

It can push Problem data to trigger the execution of a Run Book data object. It creates an RFC associated to a Problem in order to implement a fix to the issue that is documented by the Problem. It uses existing Knowledge data to solve a Problem and can create a new Knowledge data object based on Problem Management activities.

It pushes Problem data requiring emergency/specific development to the Defect functional component, and may push a Portfolio Backlog Item to the Portfolio Demand functional component for backlog processing.

Model

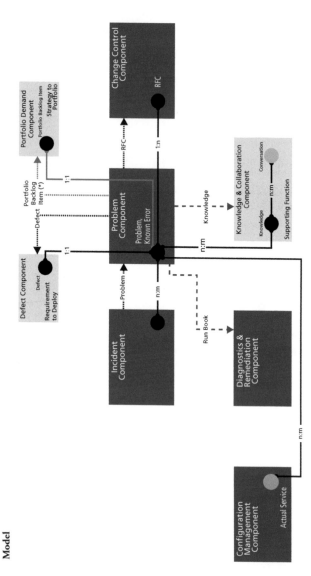

Figure 47: Problem Functional Component Level 2 Model

6.7.5 Data Architecture Criteria
The Problem functional component associates Problem(s) to Actual Service(s). It associates Incident data to the corresponding Problem record and continues the investigation around the Incident reported fault within the Problem lifecycle.

6.8 Change Control Functional Component

6.8.1 Purpose
The Change Control functional component is the system that is responsible for managing the lifecycle of all the RFCs in the IT environment. It makes sure that changes are done in a standardized way so that the business risk is minimized.

It manages change by facilitating communication with stakeholders and by assessing risk of proposed changes. Furthermore, it enables management of organizational changes and training needed for making a new release a success. Besides, it supports automation of changes so that human participation is minimized and uses a change calendar in order to avoid change conflicts.

6.8.2 Key Data Objects
The **RFC** data object records data required to manage the change lifecycle. An RFC includes details of the proposed change.

The key attributes are: RFCId, Category, SubCategory, Phase, PhaseTime, ApprovalStatus, Risk, PlannedStartTime, PlannedEndTime, Title, Description, AssignedTo, ActualServiceId.

6.8.3 Key Data Object Relationships
Fulfillment Request to RFC (1:1): Identifies the Fulfillment Request from the Fulfillment Execution functional component (R2F Value Stream) that will create an RFC on service implementation/instantiation.

RFC to Actual Service (n:m): Associates the RFC with affected Actual Service(s).

Problem, Known Error to RFC (1:n): Enables the relation of an RFC record that is created when problem resolution requires a change.

Incident to RFC (1:n): Connects RFCs to the Incidents from which they originated.

RFC to Event (n:1): Associates an Event that is available for RFC processing.

6.8.4 Functional Criteria

The Change Control functional component is the authoritative system of record for all change request information. It manages the state and lifecycle of the change. It facilitates communication with stakeholders and assesses the risk of proposed changes and their implementation. It enables management of organizational changes and training needed for making a new release a success. It may support automation of changes so that human participation is reserved for the highest added value and most complex change work.

It enables RFC management against a change calendar and avoids change collisions. It checks and steers conflict resolutions between parallel planned deployments. It can also provide change data to the Event and/ or Service Monitoring functional components in the context of change impact analysis.

6.8.5 Data Architecture Criteria

The Change Control functional component associates change(s) to Actual Service(s). It associates changes with Incidents bi-directionally (changes in response to Incidents, and changes that actually cause Incidents; i.e., unsuccessful changes).

Model

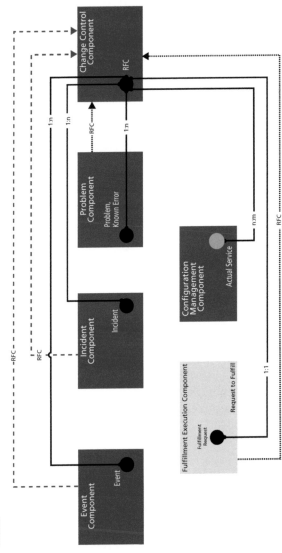

Figure 48: Change Control Functional Component Level 2 Model

It may associate changes with Events when a change triggers an Event or an Event occurs during a change period. It associates the Fulfillment Request with the RFC record as the overall framework that facilitates the IT service implementation/instantiation. It associates RFCs to the Problem in order to implement a fix to the issue that is documented by the Problem.

6.9 Configuration Management Functional Component

6.9.1 Purpose
The Configuration Management functional component is focused on tracking the inventories of Actual Services and their associated relationships. It identifies, controls, records, reports, audits, and verifies service items.

6.9.2 Key Data Objects
The **Actual Service** data object represents the realized deployment of the service. It includes CIs that represent the implemented service components.

The key attributes are: Id, Name, Type, CreateTime, LastModifiedTime, Owner, Location.

6.9.3 Key Data Object Relationships
Desired Service to Actual Service (1:1): Create traceability between the Desired and Actual Service(s).

RFC to Actual Service (n:m): Associates the RFC with affected Actual Service(s).

Problem, Known Error to Actual Service (n:m): Identifies the Actual Service to which the Problem is associated.

Run Book to Actual Service (n:m): Maps Run Book records to the associated Actual Services.

Incident to Actual Service (n:m): Identifies the Actual Service to which the Incident is associated and usually the main subject of.

Event to Actual Service (n:m): Identifies the Actual Service associated with the Event (s).

Actual Service to Service Contract (1:n): Connects the Actual Services and the Service Contract in which they are measured.

Service Monitor to Actual Service (1:n): Identifies the Actual Service being monitored.

6.9.4 Functional Criteria

The Configuration Management functional component is the system of record for all Actual Services and their associated relationships. It manages the lifecycle of the Actual Services. Moreover, it serves as the data store for the realization of the service in the production environment. It also calculates and provides the change impact based on the proposed change and the Actual Service relationships. It calculates and provides the business impact of the Incident or the Event to help in the prioritization process.

6.9.5 Data Architecture Criteria

The Configuration Management functional component allows hierarchical relationships between Actual Services. It associates a Run Book with the Actual Service against which the Run Book is associated. It associates an Actual Service with an RFC with which the change is associated. It associates the Actual Service with the Problem record against which the Problem is associated. It associates the Actual Service with the Incident with which the Incident is associated.

Model

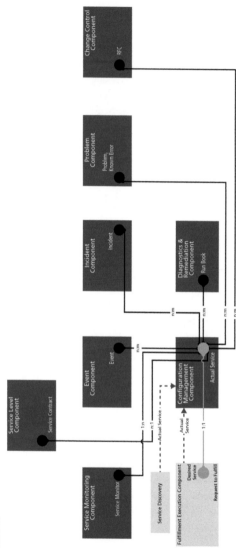

Figure 49: Configuration Management Functional Component Level 2 Model

It associates the Actual Service with the Event with which the change is associated. It associates the Actual Service with the Service Monitor with which the change is associated.

6.10 Diagnostics & Remediation Functional Component

6.10.1 Purpose

Through the use of Run Books, the Diagnostics & Remediation functional component provides diagnostics information and/or remediation steps to shorten the MTTR. Run Books help streamline diagnostics and remediation for service functions by applying knowledge solutions to service anomalies.

6.10.2 Key Data Objects

The **Run Book** data object is a routine compilation of the procedures and operations which the administrator or operator of the system carries out.

The key attributes are: ID, Description, Category, ExecutionTime, ActualServiceId.

6.10.3 Key Data Object Relationships

Actual Service to Run Book (n:m): Enables tracking Run Books and the Actual Service(s).

6.10.4 Functional Criteria

The Diagnostics & Remediation functional component is the system of record for all Run Books. It manages the Run Book lifecycle. It can allow an Event, an Incident, or a Problem to trigger a Run Book mainly for diagnostics or remediation purposes.

6.10.5 Data Architecture Criteria

The Diagnostics & Remediation functional component allows hierarchical relationships between Run Books. It associates a Run Book with an Actual Service.

Model

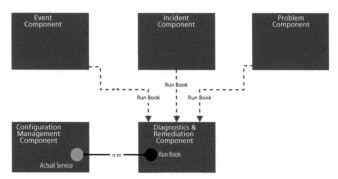

Figure 50: Diagnostics & Remediation Functional Component Level 2 Model

6.11 Service Level Functional Component

6.11.1 Purpose

The Service Level functional component enables the design, creation, and management of Service Contracts (SLAs).

6.11.2 Key Data Objects

The **Service Contract** data object describes the service characteristics and supports service measurement tracking, governance, and audit.

The key attributes are: Id, Name, Type, Provider, Consumer, StartDate, EndDate, SupportCalendar, AdherenceCalculationPeriodicity, MaintenanceWindow, ActualServiceId.

The **Key Performance Indicator** data object defines an objective that is measured, its requested threshold, and the calculation method to be used.

The key attributes are: Name, Description, Threshold.

6.11.3 Key Data Object Relationships

Service Release Blueprint to Service Contract (n:m): Identifies the Service Release Blueprint where the Service Contract templates are being stored.

Actual Service to Service Contract (1:n): Ensures functional component and data object traceability in the value stream.

Service Contract to KPI (n:m): Tracks the measurements associated with Service Contracts.

Subscription to Service Contract (1:1): Allows to trigger the instantiation of a Service Contract instance once a Subscription is instantiated.

6.11.4 Functional Criteria

The Service Level functional component is the system of record for the Service Contract. It manages the Service Contract and the KPIs lifecycle. It manages the state of the Service Contract. It manages the relations between the Service Contract data object and the KPI data object throughout their lifecycle. It receives measurements covered by the Service Contract and used for calculating KPI measurements. It creates reports on the Service Contracts.

It can receive business/IT measurements from Service Monitoring. It can instantiate a Service Contract from a Service Release Blueprint using the Service Contract (template). It may instantiate a Service Contract from a Service Contract (template) originating from the Offer Management functional component. It creates a Service Contract (instance) and

starts measuring it once a Subscription is instantiated in the Request
Rationalization functional component. It may receive Incident business
measurements from the Incident functional component, and it can send
reporting data on the Service Level status.

6.11.5 Data Architecture Criteria

The Service Level functional component allows hierarchical relationships
between Service Contracts.

Model

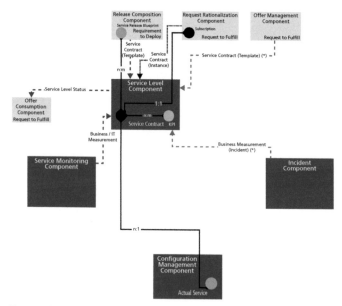

Figure 51: Service Level Functional Component Level 2 Model

6.12 Other IT Operations Area

There are other IT operations capabilities that are not part of the D2C Value Stream but have a definite relationship with it. These include, for example:

- Capacity planning will be reviewed in future releases
- Availability management will be reviewed in future releases
- Intelligence, trending, proactive alerting are within the Service Monitoring functional component

Appendix A
Differences between the IT4IT Reference Architecture and ITIL

Attribute	ITIL	IT4IT Reference Architecture
Characteristics	Process framework describing functions/capabilities/disciplines.	Information model-driven reference architecture that accommodates multiple process frameworks.
Origins	An aggregate of best practices drawn from a world-wide community of executives, managers, and individual contributors.	Driven by specific needs of Enterprise Architects and IT managers.
Form	Primarily narrative.	Primarily architectural, framed using the TOGAF standard and presented using the ArchiMate language.
Utility	Oriented to education.	Solution-orientation; usable "off-the-shelf".
Value Proposition	Enable detailed analysis at the function process level.	Enables choreography of four high-level IT value streams (Strategy to Portfolio, Requirement to Deploy, Request to Fulfill, Detect to Correct) and offers prescriptive guidance for the design of products and services that deliver them.
Structure		Mutually-exclusive and comprehensive architectural catalogs.

Attribute	ITIL	IT4IT Reference Architecture
Granularity		Precise and prescriptive representation of data and integration patterns for the whole IT management domain.
Agility	Implicit waterfall, top-down planning orientation.	Explicit accommodation of agile and DevOps trends and lean Kanban approaches.
Provenance	Evolved through various proprietary ownerships.	Dynamic, open peer-to-peer development and review processes under the aegis of The Open Group.

Appendix B
Glossary

Service Lifecycle Data Object
Data or records produced and/or consumed to advance or control the service model as it progresses through its lifecycle phases. Data objects can take a physical or digital form and are produced, consumed, or modified by functional components. Within the IT4IT Reference Architecture there are two classifications of data objects:
- Key – those that are essential to managing or advancing the service lifecycle
- Auxiliary – those that are important but not essential

IT Value Chain
A classification scheme for the set of primary and supporting activities that contribute to the overall lifecycle of creating net value of a product or service offering provided by or through the IT function. Within the IT4IT framework it is used to describe the model of the IT business function. It includes primary activities such as planning, production, consumption, fulfillment, and support. It also includes supporting activities such as finance, human resource, governance, and supplier management.

Value Chain
A classification scheme for the complete set of primary and supporting activities that contribute to the lifecycle of creating net value of a market offering. (Note: The Value Chain concept is derived from Michael Porter's book Competitive Advantage.[2])

---

2 See the referenced M. Porter: Competitive Advantage: Creating and Sustaining Superior Performance.

Value Stream
Describes the key activities for a discrete area within the IT Value Chain where some unit of net value is created or added to the service as it progresses through its lifecycle. The IT4IT framework describes four value streams (Strategy to Portfolio, Requirement to Deploy, Request to Fulfill, Detect to Correct).

Functional Component
A software building block. The smallest unit of technology in the IT4IT Reference Architecture that can stand on its own and be useful as a whole to an IT practitioner (or IT service provider). Functional components must have defined inputs and outputs that are data objects and they must have an impact on a key data object.

Service Model Backbone Data Object
Key data objects that annotate an aspect of the service model in its conceptual, logical, consumable, or physical state. These data objects and their relationships form the Service Model Backbone which provides a holistic view of a service.

Relationship
Primarily used to depict the connections between (or interactions with) data objects. In the IT4IT Reference Architecture, relationships are based on three design principles:
- System of record – used to depict the relationships used to control authoritative source data via a system-to-system interface
  These relationships are prescriptive in that they must be maintained to ensure the integrity of the IT4IT Reference Architecture.
- System of engagement – used to describe the relationships between data objects and humans or functional components via a user experience interface
- System of insight – used to describe relationships between data objects for the purpose of generating knowledge, information, or analytics

System of Record
A synonym for a system that contains and/or controls authoritative source data.

Note: This term can be easily confused with system of record relationships.

IT Service
A performance of an act that applies computing and information management competencies or resources for the benefit of another party.

IT Initiative
Any one of the class of temporary endeavors such as projects or programs with a defined beginning and end, undertaken to achieve an objective or outcome, at a specified cost.

Appendix C
Acronyms and Abbreviations

ARTS	Association for Retail Technology Standards
BIAN	Banking Industry Architecture Network
BRM	Business Risk Management
BYOD	Bring Your Own Device
CI	Configuration Item
CMMI	Capability Maturity Model Integration
COBIT	Control Objectives for Information and Related Technology
COTS	Commercial Off-The-Shelf
DevOps	Development and Operations
DML	Definitive Media Library
EMMM	Exploration, Mining, Metals & Minerals (The Open Group)
eTOM	Business Process Framework (TM Forum)
IaaS	Infrastructure as a Service
IT	Information Technology
ITIL	Information Technology Infrastructure Library
KPI	Key Performance Indicator
MTTR	Mean Time To Repair
NRF	National Retail Federation
OpEx	Operating Expenditure
PaaS	Platform as a Service
PMO	Project Management Office
QA	Quality Assurance
RFC	Request for Change
ROI	Return On Investment
SaaS	Software as a Service
SAFe	Scaled Agile Framework
SLA	Service-Level Agreement
SME	Subject Matter Expert
TCO	Total Cost of Ownership

TOSCA   Topology and Orchestration Specification for Cloud
         Applications (OASIS)
UML   Unified Modeling Language

Index